INDIANS ESSENTIAL

Everything You Need to Know to Be a Real Fan!

Mary Schmitt Boyer

TRIUMPH
BOOKS

Library of Congress Cataloging-in-Publication Data

Boyer, Mary Schmitt.
    Indians essential : everything you need to know to be a real fan! / Mary Schmitt Boyer.
      p. cm.
    Includes bibliographical references.
    ISBN-13: 978-1-57243-933-7 (alk. paper)
    ISBN-10: 1-57243-933-5 (alk. paper)
      1. Cleveland Indians (Baseball team)—History. I. Title.

GV875.C7B69 2007
796.357'640977132—dc22

                                                        2006031723

This book is available in quantity at special discounts for your group or organization. For further information, contact:

Triumph Books
542 South Dearborn Street
Suite 750
Chicago, Illinois 60605
(312) 939-3330
Fax (312) 663-3557

Printed in U.S.A.
ISBN: 978-1-57243-933-7
Design by Patricia Frey
All photos courtesy of AP/Wide World Photos except where otherwise indicated

For the men who taught me the most about baseball; my dad, Al Schmitt, a real fan, and Coach Chuck Bilek of Milwaukee Washington High School's Purgolders.

And for Gene, who watches with me now.

Contents

Foreword

755. Almost any sports fan can tell you that number represents the major league record for home runs and that Henry Aaron possesses the record. That's what makes baseball so special to millions of fans. It's the history and tradition of the game that lives on from generation to generation. An Indians fan may not remember his wedding anniversary, but he can tell you the date that Bob Feller threw Major League Baseball's only Opening Day no-hitter. An Indians fan may forget what she had for lunch on any given day, but she can vividly describe the ninth inning of Game 7 of the 1997 World Series.

In *Indians Essential,* Mary Schmitt Boyer has covered all the bases of Indians baseball—from the 1869 Cleveland Forest Citys to the present Cleveland Indians. Mary will take you on a journey that includes the thrill of the 1920 and 1948 World Series champions to the heartbreak losses in the 1954, 1995, and 1997 World Series. Relive the historical exploits of Larry Doby and Frank Robinson, as well as the beloved careers of Bob Feller, Al Rosen, and Rocky Colavito. A favorite chapter of mine is about my former partner Herb Score. Other than Bob Feller, no one has ever been more identified with or meant more to the Indians than Herb has.

Having been an Indians broadcaster since 1990, I felt I had a pretty good grasp on the Tribe's history, but Mary's book brought up many interesting facts and stories that I hadn't heard before and enjoyed learning about. It also was great fun to relive the experience of the tremendous 1990s playoff teams. So many talented players and so many special memories. An era unlike any other for Tribe fans.

History and tradition. It's what separates baseball from any other sport. It's what fans clamor for, and it's what Mary's *Indians Essential* is all about. I truly enjoyed the book and know that you, too, will enjoy this trip down memory lane. And remember Indians fans: next year is right around the corner.

—Tom Hamilton

Acknowledgments

Knowing where to start is the hard part.

Thanks to all those in the Cleveland Indians organization, particularly Mark Shapiro, Bob DiBiasio, Bart Swain, Curtis Danberg, Jeff Sibel, and Susie Giuliano, for their time and insights.

Interviewing Bob Feller was a thrill—Al Rosen, too. Russ Schneider and Terry Pluto were invaluable as well.

Thanks to the deans of baseball writers, Paul Hoynes of *The (Cleveland) Plain Dealer*, a true genius; Sheldon Ocker of the *Akron Beacon Journal*; and Jim Ingraham of the *News-Herald*, and all their colleagues, especially Andy Call of the *Canton News Repository*, who is always so helpful, and Anthony Castrovince of MLB.com. Thanks to all my colleagues at *The Plain Dealer*, especially my bosses, Roy Hewitt, Mike Starkey, and Dave Campbell; talented columnists Bill Livingston and Bud Shaw; Burt Graeff, a true pro; Bob Dolgan, who is always willing to share his vast knowledge of sports history; and Dennis Manoloff, a tireless worker who has been incredibly supportive. Thanks, too, to Patti Graziano and her staff in the *Plain Dealer* News Research department and Mary Ellen Kollar at the Cleveland Public Library. Of course, without Tom Bast and Jessica Paumier at Triumph Books, this book would not have happened.

During my research, I read all or parts of the following books: *The Cleveland Indians Encyclopedia*, Third Edition, by Russ Schneider; *Omar! My Life On and Off the Field*, by Omar Vizquel with Bob Dyer; *Omar Vizquel: The Man with the Golden Glove*, by Dennis Manoloff; *Cleveland Indians Facts & Trivia*, by Marc Davis; *Our Tribe* and *The Curse of Rocky Colavito*, by Terry Pluto; *Heroes, Scamps, and Good Guys*, by Bob Dolgan; *Legends of the Tribe*, by Morris Eckhouse;

Bob Feller's Little Black Book of Baseball Wisdom, by Bob Feller with Burton Rocks; *Me and the Spitter,* by Gaylord Perry with Bob Sudyk; *Pride against Prejudice: The Biography of Larry Doby,* by Joseph Thomas Moore; *Veeck—As in Wreck,* by Bill Veeck and Ed Linn; *Pitchin' Man Satchel Paige's Own Story,* as told to Hal Lebovitz; *Now Pitching: Bob Feller,* by Bob Feller with Bill Gilbert; *The Cleveland Indians,* by Franklin Lewis; *Don't Knock the Rock,* by Gordon Cobbledick; *Lou Boudreau: Covering All the Bases,* by Lou Boudreau with Russell Schneider; *Frank: The First Year,* by Frank Robinson with Dave Anderson; *Frank Robinson: The Making of a Man,* by Russell Schneider; and *Super Joe: The Life and Legend of Joe Charboneau,* by Burt Graeff and Terry Pluto.

Finally, thanks to Melissa Levy of Carmichael Lynch Spong and Scott Schorr of Lazy Bones Recordings.

Baseball's Beginnings in Cleveland

Baseball had a dubious beginning in Cleveland.

On June 2, 1869, the Cleveland Forest Citys lost to professional baseball's first team, the Cincinnati Red Stockings, 25–6, in Case Commons Field. The Forest Citys played in the first pro league, the National Association, until 1872, when the team disbanded.

From 1879 to 1884 Cleveland played in the National League, then joined the American Association from 1887 to 1888. In 1889 Cleveland returned to the National League, where it used the nickname Spiders, reportedly because of its many tall and skinny players. In 1890 there were even two pro baseball teams in Cleveland—one in the National League and one in the ill-fated Players League, which lasted just one year.

In 1891 future Hall of Fame pitcher Cy Young and the Spiders moved into National League Park on the corner of East 66th Street and Lexington Avenue, where they beat Cincinnati in their opener, 12–3. How times had changed. In fact, the Spiders would reach the championship series three times, beating Baltimore to win the Temple Cup in 1895.

In 1900 Byron Bancroft "Ban" Johnson, president of the Western League minor league, decided to compete against the National League. When the NL decreased from 12 teams to eight, Johnson moved his teams into the vacated NL cities, including Cleveland, and christened the new organization the American League. After one year of minor league play, the AL began major league play in 1901. This team—originally called the Bluebirds, later shortened to Blues because of the color of its uniforms—was the forerunner of the Indians of today.

The Blues actually played the first major league AL game in history, losing 8–2 at Chicago on April 24, 1901. They did win their home opener, beating Milwaukee 4–3 on April 29, but they finished the season with a 54–82 record.

By 1902 Bill Armour replaced Jimmy McAleer as manager, and the players voted to change the team's name to the more rugged Bronchos. By 1903 the team got rid of the blue uniforms and after a newspaper contest was held, the team was renamed the Naps in honor of star second baseman Napoleon Lajoie, who gave the team immediate credibility when he joined it as a player in 1902 after jumping from the National League. (Lajoie, born September 5, 1875, in Woonsocket, Rhode Island, actually switched from the NL Philadelphia Phillies to the AL Philadelphia Athletics, a move later challenged in court. The court case was thrown out, but a restraining

Cy Young, in an undated photo. The right-handed pitcher owns several virtually untouchable records, including games started (815), completed starts (749), and innings pitched (7,356).

DID YOU KNOW ... That Cleveland has had 10 player/managers in its history? According to the *Cleveland Indians Encyclopedia*, Third Edition, the 10 were Jimmy McAleer in 1901, Bill Bradley in 1905, Napoleon Lajoie from 1905 to 1909, James "Deacon" McGuire from 1909 to 1911, George Stovall in 1911, Harry Davis in 1912, Joe Birmingham from 1912 to 1914, Tris Speaker from 1919 to 1926, Lou Boudreau from 1942 to 1950, and Frank Robinson from 1975 to 1977.

order prohibited him from playing for any team in Philadelphia other than the Phillies. So when the Cleveland team visited Philadelphia the next couple of years, Lajoie did not play.)

Lajoie replaced Armour, becoming player/manager in 1905. Under Lajoie, called "Larry" by teammates unsure how to pronounce his last name, the Indians finished as high as second, with a 90–64 record in 1908, but Lajoie opted to give up managing in 1909, perhaps influenced in part by incidents like the time first baseman George Stovall hit him with a chair after being dropped in the batting order. Judging by his results, it proved to be the right decision for Lajoie. The very next season, he challenged the legendary Ty Cobb for the American League batting title and the new Chalmers automobile that came with it.

In a controversial finish, the well-liked Lajoie got eight hits in his final eight at-bats against the St. Louis Browns to finish with a .384084 batting average, compared to the despised Cobb's .384944. In the end, Cobb and Lajoie each got a car from Chalmers, while the Browns were reprimanded for their part in the finish.

Interestingly enough, in 1981 *The Sporting News* conducted a review of that batting race and found that Cobb got credit for two hits twice. Then baseball commissioner Bowie Kuhn refused to change the results, but *The Sporting News*'s record book lists Lajoie as the 1910 batting champion.

In another irony, in his book *The Cleveland Indians*, Franklin Lewis reported that Hughie Jennings, manager of the Detroit Tigers, called Indians owner Charles Somers during spring training in 1908 and offered to trade the cantankerous Cobb for outfielder Elmer Flick, an offer Somers declined.

7—Number of Indians who have led the AL in batting.

Name	Year	Batting Average
Nap Lajoie	1903	.344
Nap Lajoie	1904	.376
Elmer Flick	1905	.308
Tris Speaker	1916	.386
Lew Fonseca	1929	.369
Lou Boudreau	1944	.327
Bob Avila	1954	.341

Lajoie continued to play with the Indians through the 1914 season, and his impact is felt to this day. He leads all Indians players with 2,046 hits in his career and is second in games played with 1,614 and doubles with 424. He is third in total bases with 2,725, runs batted in with 919, and batting average at .339. He was the third player to get 3,000 hits, and his .422 average in 1901 (with Philadelphia) is still the best in the history of the American League.

Of course, with his departure in 1914, the Naps no longer seemed like an appropriate nickname for Cleveland's team, so yet another name change was in order. For years, it was believed a poll of newspaper readers selected "Indians" in honor of former Indian Louis Francis Sockalexis, a Penobscot Indian from Old Town, Maine, who starred at Holy Cross College and who became something of a cult figure after playing for the Spiders from 1897 to 1899 and batting .338 in 1897. He was the first recognized American Indian to play in the major leagues. (James Madison Toy, who debuted in the late 1880s, was half Sioux, but apparently he did not reveal his heritage at the time.)

However, research by sportswriter Bob Dolgan of *The* (Cleveland) *Plain Dealer* found that while fans were asked to send in suggestions for a new name, there was no official contest and Sockalexis was barely mentioned in stories about the new name. Instead, Somers apparently solicited suggestions from the baseball writers, who reportedly polled their readers, and "Indians" was selected. Cleveland's old National League team occasionally had been referred to as the Indians whenever Sockalexis had a good game, but Dolgan's research and that of others indicated the nickname was used derisively as well.

Sockalexis, the first member of the Holy Cross Athletic Hall of Fame who was also named to the Maine Sports Hall of Fame, remains an intriguing figure in Indians history. He is featured in a two-page spread in the team's press guide, which compares his debut in the major leagues to that of Jackie Robinson, who broke the color barrier in 1947.

Whatever the source of the new nickname, it took the Indians some time to recover from the loss of Lajoie, but by 1917 they finished third in the American League, and in 1918 and 1919 they finished second. Player/manager Tris Speaker led them to a first-place finish in 1920, and they beat the Brooklyn Dodgers five games to two to win their first World Series in what was then a best-of-nine affair.

Speaker managed for six more seasons but couldn't get the Indians back to the World Series. It wasn't until 1948 that player/manager Lou Boudreau repeated that feat, and the Indians beat the Boston Braves four games to two in a best-of-seven series to win their second World Series.

Little did baseball fans in Cleveland realize that this victory celebration would be their last for a long, long time.

Al Lopez replaced Boudreau in 1951, and in 1954 the Indians once again played in the World Series. But they were swept out in four games by the New York Giants. It would be 41 years before the Indians reached their sport's biggest stage again, losing to the Atlanta Braves in six games in 1995. The series brought renewed calls for the teams to abandon their Native American nicknames and logos, though neither did so. The Indians

TRIVIA

If Napoleon Lajoie was the third player in baseball history to get 3,000 hits, who were the first two?

Answers to the trivia questions are on pages 167–168.

also made it to the 1997 World Series, losing in seven games to the Florida Marlins.

In the Indians' colorful history, there were thrilling victories and heart-wrenching losses, triumphs and tragedies, rising stars and wily veterans. Two of the team's proudest moments came when Larry Doby became the first African American player in the American League in 1947 and Frank Robinson became the first African American manager in 1975. The team, which began play in cozy League Park and then moved to cavernous Cleveland Municipal Stadium, opened a beautiful new park, Jacobs Field, in 1994.

Their loyal fans followed them every step of the way, believing in their hearts that one day soon the Indians would once again hoist that World Series championship trophy to the skies.

A Great Player, a Great Manager

It is safe to say that Tris Speaker was not overjoyed when he learned the Boston Red Sox were planning to trade him to the Cleveland Indians. He told General Manager Bob McRoy he would not report.

"I think you've got a bad ballclub, for one thing," he told McRoy. "You finished seventh and eighth in two years. Cleveland isn't a good baseball town, either. Boston is great, and it looks like we might win another pennant there. I don't want to go to Cleveland and wind up in the second division."

Unfortunately for Speaker, the deal was already done. The Indians sent pitcher Sam Jones, infielder Fred Thomas, and $55,000 to the Red Sox for the great center fielder on April 12, 1916.

Speaker brought the trade on himself. After batting .322 as the Red Sox won the 1915 World Series, he was expecting a hefty raise over the $9,000 he made that season. But when Boston owner Joe Lannin sent him a new contract for the same $9,000 Speaker made in 1915, Speaker, seeking $15,000, was outraged and skipped the start of spring training.

Ed Bang, sports editor of the *Cleveland Press,* saw that story on the wire and called McRoy. Bang told McRoy he knew Lannin, and he knew Lannin would sell any player, including Speaker.

So the Indians got the services of an eventual Hall of Fame outfielder for the next 11 years and a field general who would lead them to the 1920 World Series championship. Not a bad deal.

Speaker was born in Hubbard, Texas, on April 4, 1888. Almost 6' tall, he was a real-life cowboy who could ride and rope with the best of them. Eventually he turned his athleticism to baseball, starting as a right-handed pitcher. When he broke his right arm, he

Manager Tris Speaker at spring training in Lakeland, Florida, on March 11, 1926.

threw left-handed before finally moving to the outfield. He knocked around the minor leagues in Cleburne, Texas, and Houston before the Red Sox bought his contract for $750. After a false start with the Red Sox in 1907, when he batted just .158 in seven games, he returned to the minor leagues. But he rejoined the Red Sox in

TRIVIA

How did Manager Tris Speaker surprise onlookers after the Indians won the 1920 World Series?

Answers to the trivia questions are on pages 167–168.

1908 and became a star, winning the Chalmers Award (precursor to the Most Valuable Player award) with a .383 batting average and 10 home runs in 1912 as the Red Sox won the World Series. Though his home-run totals fell off, he batted .363, .338, and .322 the next three seasons, and the Red Sox won the World Series again in 1915.

That wasn't good enough for Lannin, but it was more than good enough for the Indians. Despite balking at moving to Cleveland, Speaker led the American League with a .386 batting average in 1916. In fact, he would hit .300 or better in 10 of his 11 seasons in Cleveland. On July 18, 1919, he replaced Lee Fohl as the team's manager. He would lead the Indians to a 617–520 record (a .543 winning percentage) in the next eight seasons, batting .388 with 107 RBIs in the championship season of 1920.

Nicknamed "Spoke" as a play on words of his last name or "the Gray Eagle" because of his gray hair, he presented an imposing figure. He was a tough, demanding player, and he did not change as a manager. Before Game 3 of the 1920 World Series, he and pitcher Duster Mails shared a cab to Ebbets Field. Mails, a nervous sort who had somehow managed to put together a seven-game winning streak, told Speaker he could pitch that day, so Speaker named him the starter. But after they arrived at the ballpark, Mails sent word he couldn't pitch, claiming his arm was sore. Ray Caldwell volunteered to start but got in trouble early, whereupon Speaker sent to the bullpen for Mails, whose warm-up pitches had looked (and sounded) great.

"You haven't got any sore arm," a seething Speaker told Mails. "You told me this morning you wanted to pitch. Now you pitch, and you pitch with everything you've got in you." Mails got the next two batters out to end the inning, but the Indians couldn't come back and lost Game 3, 2–1, giving the Brooklyn Dodgers a two-games-to-one lead in the best-of-nine series.

Of course, Caldwell and Speaker had their own weird history. A known drinker, Caldwell had been released by the Red Sox late in the 1919 season. Speaker always liked him, though, and gave him another chance while inserting the most curious clause into his contract. The contract insisted Caldwell get drunk after every game he pitched, stay away from the ballpark the next day, report to Speaker the day after that, and be ready to pitch every fourth day. Whether he followed the deal to the letter isn't known, but Caldwell went 5–1 the rest of the season and pitched a no-hitter on September 10 against the Yankees in New York.

Speaker was the toast of the town after the Indians won the World Series, but he tore ligaments in his knee on September 11, 1921, ending any hopes of a repeat for the defending champions. Still, until his final season as a player in 1926, he continued to be a stellar fielder and batted no less than .304. He finished his 22 seasons with a .345 batting average, fifth best in history. His 792 doubles are the most in history, his 3,514 hits are the fifth most in history, and his 1,882 runs are the 11th most in history.

In spite of those numbers, however, Speaker's career ended on a sour note. In 1926, retired Detroit pitcher Dutch Leonard accused Speaker, Ty Cobb, and Smoky Joe Wood of fixing a game and betting on it in 1919. Leonard reportedly resented the way he'd been treated when Cobb was the Tigers manager. Supposedly the Indians, who had already clinched second place, let the Tigers win a game late in the season in order to assure that they would finish in third place and earn a share of the World Series payout. Leonard produced letters affirming all this and sent them to baseball commissioner Kenesaw Mountain Landis. Landis eventually cleared the players, but American League president Ban Johnson made them retire as player/managers.

Speaker played two more years, with Washington and Philadelphia, before retiring after the 1928 season. He did return to the Indians as an outfield instructor and helped groom Larry Doby, the first black player in the American League.

Speaker died December 8, 1958, of a heart attack at age 70.

1920: From Tragedy to Triumph

Truth be told, it never looked as if 1920 was going to be the Indians' year.

Instead, it appeared it would be best remembered for the tragic death of shortstop Ray Chapman, who was hit in the head by a pitch from Carl Mays of the Yankees on August 16 in New York and died the next day—the only major league player ever fatally wounded during a game.

But the Indians regrouped, first using reserve infielder Harry Lunte and then calling up Joe Sewell from the minor leagues when Lunte hurt his leg, and continued to push toward the postseason. They had finished second to Boston and Chicago, respectively, in 1918 and 1919, and player/manager Tris Speaker had them one game ahead of Chicago in the last week of the 1920 regular season when seven players on the defending champion White Sox were suspended for conspiring to fix the 1919 World Series. Cleveland won three of its last five games and finished two games ahead of Chicago, setting up a best-of-nine World Series against the Brooklyn Dodgers. Sewell, not on the roster September 1, won an appeal to be able to play. The series was to have started in Cleveland, but renovations to the ballpark now called Dunn Field in honor of new team president Jim Dunn were not completed in time, so the first games were moved to Brooklyn.

Game 1, Tuesday, October 5. Cleveland 3, at Brooklyn 1— Catcher Steve O'Neill had two doubles and two runs batted in to back the five-hit pitching of Stan Coveleski on a cold and windy day before a chilled crowd of 23,573 in Ebbets Field. Coveleski walked just one and held the Dodgers scoreless through six innings.

DID YOU KNOW . . . That the Dodgers of the 1920s were sometimes called the Robins in honor of Manager Wilbert Robinson?

"Coveleski pitched excellent ball today," Speaker told reporters after the game. "With the wind blowing as hard as it was, he worked under a handicap but he delivered in the pinches, and that is what counts. He was never nervous. It was just a ball game with him. He pitched a typical Coveleski game.

"The result of the game goes to show that I was not boasting when I contended that Cleveland would display just as good pitching as Brooklyn. They would have us believe that Brooklyn has the real pitching market cornered. It is my belief that the pitching in the American League is every bit as good as that in the National, and our batting average of .302 [for the regular season] was deservedly earned."

Game 2, Wednesday, October 6. At Brooklyn 3, Cleveland 0— Burleigh Grimes held the Indians scoreless and didn't allow a runner past second base until the eighth inning as the Dodgers evened the series before a crowd of 22,559.

"I give Grimes the credit," Speaker told reporters after the game. "He is a good pitcher. He has a great spitball."

Game 3, Thursday, October 7. At Brooklyn 2, Cleveland 1— The Dodgers jumped on Ray Caldwell for two runs in the first inning, and left-hander Sherry Smith limited Cleveland to three hits. The Indians scored their only run when Speaker raced home from second after his double rolled through the legs of left fielder Zach Wheat in the fourth inning.

"The clubs are very evenly matched, but I think we have the edge on Cleveland in respect to pitchers," Brooklyn manager Wilbert "Uncle Robbie" Robinson told reporters after the game. "The thing needed in a World Series is nerve, and our boys certainly have plenty of it."

Game 4, Saturday, October 9. At Cleveland 5, Brooklyn 1— This time it was the Indians' turn to jump out to a quick lead. Brooklyn right-hander Leon Cadore found himself trailing 2–0 in the first inning, and another five-hitter by Coveleski helped the Indians knot the series and provided a successful outcome in the first World Series game to be played in Cleveland.

"From the start, I never had any doubt of our being able to win the championship of the world," Tris Speaker told reporters after Game 7 of the 1920 World Series against the Brooklyn Dodgers.

Game 5, Sunday, October 10. At Cleveland 8, Brooklyn 1—It was quite a day for the Indians and their fans. Bill Wambsganss made the only unassisted triple play in World Series history, pitcher Jim Bagby became the first pitcher to hit a home run in the World Series, and Elmer Smith became the first player to hit a grand-slam home run in the World Series as the Indians, behind Smith's first-inning blast off Grimes, routed the Dodgers.

The Dodgers had runners on first and second in the fifth inning when pitcher Clarence Mitchell, who relieved Grimes, lined a shot toward center field. Wambsganss caught it, stepped on second to double up Pete Kilduff, and then tagged out Otto Miller as he approached second base.

"It was one of the most remarkable games I ever took part in," Speaker told reporters after the game. "I am especially proud of Bill Wambsganss. I am happy for his sake. I trust what he did yesterday will silence the criticism of him forever. Bill is a great player. Any team in the country would be glad to have him."

Game 6, Monday, October 11. At Cleveland 1, Brooklyn 0— Walter "Duster" Mails pitched his way out of a bases-loaded jam in the second inning and threw a three-hitter as the Indians moved within a game of their first World Series championship. Cleveland scored its only run on a two-out single by Speaker in the sixth inning and a double by George Burns.

Game 7, Tuesday, October 12. At Cleveland 3, Brooklyn 0— Coveleski tied a major league record by recording his third victory in one World Series, and the Indians shut out the Dodgers for the second straight game to win their first baseball championship before a deliriously happy crowd of 27,525 at League Park. The Indians got the only run they needed in the fourth inning, on a throwing error by Grimes, who was working on only two days' rest. They tacked on single runs in the fifth and seventh. At the end of the game, fans swarmed onto the field to celebrate.

"From the start, I never had any doubt of our being able to win the championship of the world," Speaker told reporters after the game. "The American League campaign was what gave us the trouble, but the fact that we had to fight it right out to the finish helped us against Brooklyn. We were playing at top speed when the regular season ended and kept going the same gait until we had won the world's title.

"All the boys have felt the same way. They know they are a good ballclub and have known it right along. When we lost two in a row in Brooklyn, none of us was discouraged for we knew we had a better ballclub than Brooklyn and would win if all the breaks were not against us."

Robinson told reporters after the game, "Cleveland has a wonderful ballclub, and Tris Speaker and his men certainly deserve the splendid support they have received from the city. It was a well-fought and honestly played series. We did our best, but we couldn't hit Cleveland pitching."

The players each got a new contract and a bonus worth 10 days' pay, and Speaker got an engraved gold watch. The players gave the owner diamond-studded cuff links.

A Walk through the Parks

When people describe Russ Schneider as a walking encyclopedia of Indians knowledge, they mean it.

Schneider, a longtime sportswriter and columnist for *The (Cleveland) Plain Dealer,* wrote the book on the Indians—several of them, in fact—including *The Cleveland Indians Encyclopedia,* Third Edition. He also wrote *Frank Robinson: The Making of a Manager, Lou Boudreau: Covering All the Bases, The Boys of the Summer of '48, Tales from the Tribe Dugout, More Tales from the Tribe Dugout, Tribe Memories, The Glorious Indian Summer of 1995,* and *The Unfulfilled Indian Summer of 1996.*

A graduate of Cleveland's West Tech High School, Schneider signed a minor league contract with the Indians as a catcher in 1949 and played in the team's farm system before becoming a sports-writer and eventually covering the team for 14 years. He also served as the team's official scorer for 21 seasons.

Over the course of his life, he spent time in each of the ballparks that housed the Indians—League Park, Cleveland Municipal Stadium, and Jacobs Field. Each held special memories for him—if for no other reason than they provided sites for the game he loves.

"I enjoyed them all," Schneider said. "It's the ballgames I enjoy."

League Park opened in 1891 on the corner of Lexington Avenue and East 66th Street. It was a cozy little all-wood ballpark with no lights. The 40-foot-high right-field fence was just 290 feet from home plate. It was 375 feet to left field and 460 feet to center field, although a 1909 renovation shortened that to 420 feet and increased the seating capacity from 9,000 to 23,000, including the bleachers. According to Schneider's *Encyclopedia,* the weird dimensions were a

That nine no-hitters were pitched in Cleveland Municipal Stadium? Six of them were by Indians pitchers—Len Barker (May 15, 1981), Don Black (July 10, 1947), Dick Bosman (July 19, 1974), Dennis Eckersley (May 30, 1977), Bob Feller (July 1, 1951), and Sonny Siebert (June 10, 1966). The others were by Minnesota's Dean Chance (August 25, 1967), the New York Yankees' Allie Reynolds (July 12, 1951), and Toronto's Dave Stieb (September 2, 1990).

games (and other events, like concerts by the Beatles and Rolling Stones), there were plenty of complaints about the drafty stadium situated on the edge of Lake Erie.

In 1928 voters approved a $2.5 million bond issue to finance construction. Three years later, the doors opened on the $3 million facility. Its two decks could hold 78,189 people. It was 470 feet straightaway to center field, though that distance was shortened to 400 feet in 1947. A total of 36,936 turned out for the opening event— a heavyweight title fight in which champion Max Schmeling beat Young Stribling with a 15th-round technical knockout on July 3, 1931.

The Indians started playing some games there in 1932, played their whole 1933 season there, and then split time at League Park when attendance fell off. Obviously, in 60 years there were many, many memorable moments—like the home run awarded to Carlos Martinez when the ball bounced off the head of Texas outfielder Jose Canseco's head on May 26, 1993—and many, many forgettable ones. However, the Stadium never really provided much of a home-field advantage. In 60 seasons the Indians' record in the Stadium was 2,234–1,951 (.534).

Much history was made there, including Frank Robinson's debut as the first African American manager on April 8, 1975. Joe DiMaggio's 56-game hitting streak came to an end there on July 17, 1941, thanks to two great stops by Ken Keltner and another by shortstop Lou Boudreau, who wouldn't let a bad hop stop him from making a play. Pitcher Herb Score got hit in the eye there by a ball off the bat of Gil McDougald on May 7, 1957, ending a promising playing career. But the most infamous game may have come on June 4, 1974, when a riot fueled by 10-Cent Beer Night forced a forfeit to the Texas Rangers.

By the **NUMBERS**

Jacobs Field

Left field: 325 feet

Center field: 405 feet

Right Field: 325 feet

Height of fence in center and right: 9 feet

Suites: 122

Seats: 43,315

Light towers: 19

Cost: $169 million

Though it was considered a palace when it opened in 1931, it did not age well over the years. In spite of facelifts in 1967 and 1974, the "Mistake on the Lake" became the butt of jokes by players and fans tired of battling the winds and the gnats. Though many fans will remember good days, there was a lot of bad baseball played there—most of it in front of thousands of empty seats.

Schneider, though, had a special affection for the place he worked as a reporter and official scorer.

"I liked the Stadium," said Schneider, who was a boy in the crowd the day DiMaggio's hitting streak was stopped. "But I didn't have to endure it as a spectator."

The Indians and the Browns inhabited the Stadium full-time from 1947 to 1993, ending an era with a 4–0 loss to the Chicago White Sox on October 3, 1993, in front of 72,454 loyal and nostalgic fans.

Six months later the Indians opened their jewel of a new ballpark, Jacobs Field, at the intersection of Ontario Street and Carnegie Avenue.

"What more could you ask for?" said Schneider, who had spent many hours photographing the construction of the facility.

Shortstop Omar Vizquel, obtained in a trade from Seattle in the off-season, was making his Cleveland debut the day Jacobs Field opened.

"When I first saw Jacobs Field a few days before the 1994 season opener, it knocked my socks off," Vizquel said in his 2002 autobiography, *Omar! My Life On and Off the Field* with Bob Dyer. "Everything was first class. There wasn't one single feature that stood out; rather, it was the overall feel. It didn't remind me of any other ballpark; it was unique. It was just a beautiful place to play ball."

The park changed the landscape of downtown Cleveland, literally and figuratively. The Indians had been unhappy in the stadium for years, feuding constantly with either the city or Cleveland Browns owner Art Modell, whose Stadium Corporation took over operation of the stadium. In 1984 Cuyahoga County voters rejected a property tax increase to fund a new domed stadium. But the Indians' new owners, brothers Dick and David Jacobs, worked with civic leaders to come up with a plan for a public/private partnership that would result in a new baseball-only stadium, as well as a new basketball arena for the Cleveland Cavaliers. The Gateway Sports and Entertainment Complex, funded in part by a sin tax on cigarettes and alcohol, helped revitalize downtown Cleveland, although the Indians' departure from the stadium hastened the departure of the Browns for Baltimore after the 1995 season.

The Browns were the furthest thing from anyone's mind when the $169 million Jacobs Field opened with much fanfare in April 1994. Although the public got its first look on April 2, when the Indians played host to the Pittsburgh Pirates in an exhibition game, the official grand opening came on April 4 in the season opener against the Seattle Mariners. President Bill Clinton threw out the first pitch, and although Randy Johnson threw a no-hitter for seven innings, the Indians eventually thrilled the 41,259 fans in attendance with a 4–3 victory on a single by Wayne Kirby in the eleventh inning.

Many thrills followed, including the 1995 and 1997 World Series, and the 1997 All-Star Game. Fans swarmed to see the team, and the team set a major league record with 455 sellouts from June 7, 1995, to April 2, 2001.

Starry, Starry Nights

Cleveland has been host to a major league record five All-Star Games in two different stadiums. Four of them were held in Cleveland Municipal Stadium, while the last was held in Jacobs Field.

Here's a review of each and comments from those involved.

July 8, 1935. American League 4, National League 1—When 69,831 fans turned out for the third All-Star Game, they set a record that would stand for almost 50 years.

Philadelphia's Jimmie Foxx hit a two-run home run off Cardinals left-hander Bill Walker in the first inning to start the AL on its way to its third straight victory. New York's Lefty Gomez and local hero Mel Harder kept the NL in check. The Indians also were represented by Joe Vosmik.

"Foxx just about wrecked the game with that homer in the first," NL manager Frankie Frisch told reporters after the game. "The turning point came with only two out in the first inning, and you can't win 'em much quicker than that."

Frisch, the Cardinals' manager, defended the decision to start Walker instead of ace Hal Schumacher of the New York Giants.

"I thought it was the best strategy at the moment," he said. "I'd start him again under the same circumstances. The only mistake he made was that home-run ball he threw to Foxx."

Frisch also said Walker had one of the few fresh arms on the NL staff.

"Practically all of them have been working hard lately, and three of the boys we had to rely on pitched nine innings yesterday. The result was they just didn't do their stuff. We had a couple of chances

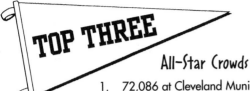

All-Star Crowds

1. 72,086 at Cleveland Municipal Stadium on August 9, 1981
2. 69,831 at Cleveland Municipal Stadium on July 8, 1935
3. 68,751 at Cleveland Municipal Stadium on July 13, 1954

to win the game with a hit in the right place, but Gomez and Harder bore down and we didn't get 'em."

Babe Ruth, who had played in his last major league game earlier that season for the Boston Braves, watched the game from a box seat on the first-base side of the field.

July 13, 1954. American League 11, National League 9—In a wild slugfest, Nellie Fox of the Chicago White Sox hit a broken-bat single over second base with two out and the bases loaded in the eighth inning to drive in the winning two runs. The game set records for hits (31) and runs (20) by two teams in an All-Star Game. There were six home runs, four by the AL.

Cleveland's Al Rosen had two of them and five RBIs, tying the All-Star Game records. Teammates Bobby Avila, who had three hits, and Larry Doby, who hit one home run, combined with Rosen for eight RBIs.

Ironically, before the game, Rosen told AL manager Casey Stengel he didn't think he'd be much help. When Rosen, who had fractured his right index finger on May 25, struck out and stranded two runners in the first, it appeared he was right.

"I didn't sleep hardly a wink last night, and when I got up this morning, the finger hurt worse than ever," Rosen told reporters after the game. "After batting practice, I told Casey that I hadn't been doing my team much good and didn't think I would do much for this one. I told him to take me out any time he felt like it. The fans voted me into the game, and I wanted to start, but I figured I'd be out of there after one time at bat. Probably would have, too, if it hadn't been for that strikeout. I couldn't leave after that. I wanted one more crack at it."

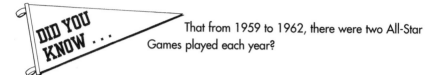

That from 1959 to 1962, there were two All-Star Games played each year?

Said Stengel to reporters after the game, "There wasn't any question of Rosen not starting, but he says that it might be a good idea to pull him out of there after his first swings. I asked the commissioner [Ford Frick], and he says it's okay if he don't go three innings like they're supposed to, but we'll have to tell you guys [reporters] all about it.

"He comes back after that strikeout and doesn't say anything, and I don't say anything either. Sure, he strikes out, but he's swinging good and I want him in there. Then he hits the home run and I look down the bench and tell [possible replacement Mickey] Vernon to relax. I see this guy's gonna be in there for a while."

Stengel was thrilled with the victory but worried about the stiff competition his Yankees would face the rest of the season.

"Now they see what I'm up against in this American League," Stengel told reporters after the game. "Your Cleveland guys sure did a job...and how about that little Fox. He gets the hit when we need it. That reminds me, though, of all those games we got left with Chicago."

July 9, 1963. National League 5, American League 3—Willie Mays went 1-for-3 with two RBIs, two runs scored, two stolen bases, one walk, and one great basket catch, despite catching his foot in the center-field fence.

"I don't care where you are, Mays always helps you win it," NL manager Alvin Dark told reporters after the game. "He'll always figure out something."

Said Mays to reporters after the game, "I love to play ball, and I want to win. Maybe it looks different to you, but I'm telling you how it is with me."

His base hit was his 20th in an All-Star Game, tying the record set by Stan Musial.

"When I'm playing, I don't have time to worry about the records," Mays told reporters.

Though he received treatment on his foot in the training room, he said there was nothing to worry about.

"Man, this fence you got fools you," Mays told reporters after the game. "In our league, we got a warning track. You can tell when you're coming to it. I got to the fence today quicker than I thought. My foot got underneath it, I guess...it's okay now."

August 9, 1981. National League 5, American League 4—The game was pushed back because of a 50-day strike by the players, but the record crowd of 72,086 fans who welcomed them back for the game that kicked off the second half of the season didn't seem to mind one bit.

MVP Gary Carter of Montreal hit two home runs, and Philadelphia's Mike Schmidt hit a two-run home run off Milwaukee's Rollie Fingers in the eighth inning as the NL rallied from a 4–3 deficit for its 10th straight victory and 18th in 19 years.

"I just had nothing," Fingers told reporters after the game. "Everything was inside and in the dirt. The ball to Schmidt just said 'Hit me' all over it."

The Indians were represented by Len Barker, who had pitched a perfect game earlier that season; Manager Dave Garcia, who coached first base; and catcher Bob Diaz. Barker, snubbed as a starter by AL manager Jim Frey in favor of Detroit's Jack Morris, retired all six batters he faced in the third and fourth innings. He also got a kiss from the notorious Morganna Roberts, better known as the Kissing Bandit.

"This was great," Barker told reporters, referring to the game and not the kiss. "The fans were outstanding. It is a pleasure to play with these guys because you know they are a great bunch of ballplayers. I can't say enough about Cleveland and the Cleveland organization. They've been behind me all the way.

"I'm not sorry I didn't start. Jack Morris deserved to start. I'm just happy to be a part of this. The players held up well, although the National League made a couple of errors. But those are part of the game."

Vice President George Bush threw out the first pitch.

July 8, 1997. American League 3, National League 1—Sandy Alomar Jr. of the Indians was the hero, but the beautiful 3-year-old Jacobs Field was the star of the 68th All-Star Game. With the score tied at 1–1 and two outs in the seventh inning, Alomar hit a two-run home run to snap a three-game losing streak by the American League and send most of the stadium-record crowd of 44,945 home happy. Alomar was named the game's MVP in a vote of the media. He is the first Indian to win the award, and the only player to do so in his home park. He was the first Indian to hit a homer in the All-Star Game since Rocky Colavito did it in 1959.

Fireworks explode over Jacobs Field prior to the start of the 68th All-Star Game on July 8, 1997.

Indians manager Mike Hargrove, Alomar, Jim Thome, and David Justice represented Cleveland. Former Indian Kenny Lofton, now with the Atlanta Braves, played for the National League. Former Indian Albert Belle of the Chicago White Sox, booed mercilessly by the fans during his introduction, was named to the AL team but chose not to play.

Alomar, leading the American League with a .375 average and a 30-game hitting streak, was a reserve on the team, so he had only one at-bat. He made the most of it, lining a 2–2 pitch off loser Shawn Estes on into the left-field bleachers. Bernie Williams, who walked and took second on a wild pitch, scored ahead of Alomar. Alomar's homer made a winner of Jose Rosado.

"I felt like I was flying," Alomar told reporters after the game. "I've never run the bases so fast on a home run. This is a dream I don't want to wake up from. You probably only get one chance to play an All-Star Game in your home stadium."

TRIVIA

Which Indians player was named to the All-Star team the most times?

Answers to the trivia questions are on pages 167–168.

Said Estes to reporters after the game, "I kept his hitting streak alive. I wouldn't have picked anybody to hit a homer off me, but I'm happy for him that he did. It's a great time for him. Playing at home, the hitting streak, the fans obviously love him."

Mel Harder: A Long and Prosperous Career

Indians fans have been fortunate to have a number of fine players stay with the team their whole careers. A few have gone from the field to the coaching ranks and increased the length of their stays. But when it comes to longevity, no one compares to Mel Harder. Harder, who died in 2002 at the age of 93, pitched for the Indians from 1928 until 1947. For the next 16 years, he served as the team's pitching coach, one of the first men named to that position.

He wore the Indians uniform for 36 years, unheard of in these days of free agency, when five years is a long time for any one player to remain with any one team. He appeared in more games (582) than any other Indians player—and won more games (223) than anyone except Bob Feller (266). As *Plain Dealer* reporter Bob Dolgan noted in Harder's obituary, his career stretched from the days of Ty Cobb and Babe Ruth to Rocky Colavito. He played for five managers and coached for seven more. (Lou Boudreau is the only manager he pitched and coached for.)

He pitched in the first game at Cleveland Municipal Stadium in 1932 and then threw out the first pitch in Jacobs Field in 1994, 62 years later.

Ironically, there was a point in 1941 when it appeared his pitching career was over. The Indians actually released him after he went 5–4. But after having surgery to remove four bone chips, he won back his job in 1942 and stayed another six years before joining the coaching ranks. Until 1963, he influenced every great pitcher the Indians had, including Feller, Bob Lemon, Herb Score, and Early Wynn. His 1954 pitching staff of Feller, Lemon, Wynn, Mike Garcia, Art

DID YOU KNOW . . . That Mel Harder was 3–0 as a manager, having been named on an interim basis for one game at the end of the 1961 season and two at the end of the 1962 season?

Houtteman, Hal Newhouser, Don Mossi, and Ray Narleski is considered the best in the history of baseball.

"He helped me most by just talking," Feller told Dolgan.

"His word was gospel," Lemon added.

When he arrived in Cleveland in 1928, he looked as if he might not last long. Born October 15, 1909, in Beemer, Nebraska, the 18-year-old was 6'1" but weighed about 140 pounds. In his book *The Cleveland Indians,* Franklin Lewis described Harder as "a right-handed pitcher of high-school age who looked as if he might fit into a jumbo-size straw if you could cut off his shock of hair." Early on, Harder told reporters he drank malted milks to bulk up. Later, he told them he'd really had a couple beers after each game.

No matter his weight—or how he increased it—his right arm was magical, and his curve ball was one of the best in the history of the game. For 11 straight seasons, from 1930 to 1940, he won 11 or more games a season, including 20 in 1934 and 22 in 1935. He was an All-Star in 1934, 1935, 1936, and 1937 and never gave up an earned run in the 13 innings he pitched—the only man who can make that claim.

The great Joe DiMaggio hit only .180 in his career against Harder, and DiMaggio and Ted Williams called Harder the toughest pitcher they ever faced, according to the *Cleveland Indians Encyclopedia,* Third Edition.

Such was Harder's stature that Manager Roger Peckinpaugh named him to pitch the opening game in Cleveland's Municipal Stadium in 1932. Before a crowd of 80,000, the three-time American League champion Philadelphia Athletics, featuring Lefty Grove, Jimmie Foxx, Al Simmons, and Mickey Cochrane, beat Harder, 1–0.

TRIVIA

Who are the only two pitchers to play longer for one team than Mel Harder, who played 20 seasons with the Indians?

Answers to the trivia questions are on pages 167–168.

Pitching coach Mel Harder playfully checks the muscles of his staff prior to the 1955 season. Photo courtesy of Bettmann/CORBIS.

In his career, he finished with a 223–186 record with 181 complete games, 25 shutouts, 23 saves, and 1,161 strikeouts. He led the Indians in innings pitched four times, wins five times, ERA four times, strikeouts three times, and complete games two times. He remains in the team's all-time top 10 in innings pitched (3426.1), shutouts, wins, and strikeouts. He also was a decent hitter, with a .165 lifetime average, and a good fielder, leading the AL in putouts four times. He was the Indians Man of the Year in 1961, the only coach so honored.

Despite all that, Harder was shunned by the Hall of Fame. When he found out in 2000 that he had not been selected again, he told Dolgan, "It's disappointing, but the more I think about it, I'm just lucky to be alive. I've been through too many rough things to worry about it."

Such an even disposition and gentlemanly manner made him popular with all those who knew him. The *Plain Dealer*'s Bill Livingston wrote a touching tribute in a column on Harder shortly after his death.

"Mel Harder belongs in the Hall of Fame for people, as well as for baseball.... But if the people from Cooperstown never called, it was their loss....

"He was, like Bob Feller...one of the treasures of this old baseball town. Mel Harder connected us to a past many of us only read or dreamed about. When you were around him, it was always summer and the Tribe was usually playing two."

Earl Averill:
All He Did Was Hit

Of the six players who have had their uniform numbers retired by the Indians, Earl Averill may be the least well known to newer or younger Indians fans.

But the fact of the matter is that in 2006, 67 years after his last season in Cleveland, Averill still is in the top 10 in 13 of 14 career batting categories for the team. He heads the Indians all-time lists in runs (1,154), triples (121), total bases (3,200), RBIs (1,084), and extra-base hits (724). He is second in at-bats (5,909), third in hits (1,903) and doubles (377), fourth in home runs (226) and walks (725), sixth in batting average (.322) and slugging percentage (.542), and eighth in games (1,509).

All the man did was hit. Left-handed, by the way.

Averill was born Howard Earl Averill in Snohomish, Washington, on May 21, 1902. His father died when Averill was two years old, and his mother, Annie, was a cook who raised three children. Averill played in Snohomish and Bellingham, Washington, before moving to the Pacific Coast League with the San Francisco Seals, who were considered to have the best outfield in the minor leagues with Averill, Roy Johnson, and Smead Jolley.

In his book *The Cleveland Indians,* Franklin Lewis wrote, "Averill was the smallest of the three with an odd batting stance, stood with his feet close, crowded the plate, swung his bat with his body instead of stepping into the pitch with a snap of the wrists."

Still, Indians general manager Billy Evans paid the Seals $50,000 for Averill in the winter of 1929, and Averill insisted he get a $5,000 bonus in the process.

Not everybody was immediately impressed with the 5'9", 172-pound Averill, nicknamed "the Rock" or "the Earl of Snohomish."

Indians owner Alva Bradley reportedly took one look at him and said, "We paid all that money for a midget?"

Then Bradley went out and, in his first at-bat with the team, hit a home run on April 16, 1929, against Detroit. From that point on, he never stopped hitting. He also became the league's best center fielder and was named to the first six All-Star Games. In the 1937 All-Star Game, he hit a line drive that broke the big toe of St. Louis pitcher Dizzy Dean.

That was just one hit, though. Averill had many, many more in a number of great seasons, starting with his rookie season when he batted .332. In 1931 he batted .333 with 209 hits and scored an

Earl Averill (front row, sixth from the left) poses with his American League teammates before the 1933 All-Star Game in Chicago.

7—Number of Indians who have hit for the cycle.

Bill Bradley, September 24, 1903, at Washington

Earl Averill, August 17, 1933, versus Philadelphia

Odell Hale, July 12, 1938, at Washington

Larry Doby, June 4, 1952, at Boston

Tony Horton, July 2, 1970, at Baltimore

Andre Thornton, April 22, 1978, at Boston

Travis Hafner, August 14, 2003, at Minnesota

Indians single-season-record 140 runs, with 32 home runs and 143 RBIs. In 1933 he became the second Indian to hit for the cycle on August 17 against Philadelphia.

His string of six straight seasons in which he hit .300 or better came to an end in 1935, when he suffered burns from a firecracker on his forehead, chest, and right hand. He missed six weeks after the accident on June 26, 1935, and batted .288 in 140 games that season.

But he came back strong the next year. In 1936 he led the league with 232 hits, tied for the league lead with 15 triples, and batted .378. Incredibly his numbers did not lead the American League. He finished second to Luke Appling, who batted .388.

After that season, Averill demanded a $2,000 raise, which did not sit well with Bradley. Eventually Averill agreed to a $1,000 raise (to $15,000) and a $2,000 bonus if he had a good year in 1937. But when he batted .299 in 1937, Bradley refused to pay the bonus. Averill came back and hit .330 in 1938, but when he dipped to .273 in 1939, Bradley traded him to Detroit on June 14 for pitcher Harry Eisenstat and cash. Averill batted .262 with Detroit that season and .280 in 1940. But the Tigers released him after that season. He signed with the Boston Braves in 1941, but after batting .188 in eight games, he was released.

After he retired he returned to Snohomish and ran a motel and a flower shop. He was elected to the Hall of Fame in 1975, the same year the Indians retired his No. 3.

The Greatest Indian

Bob Feller has one rule of thumb.

"You never want to leave your house or your hotel room without a couple pens in your pocket," the Hall of Famer said, laughing.

Seventy years after Feller made his debut as a 17-year-old hotshot with the Indians on August 23, 1936, he is more popular than ever. In July 2006, the U.S. House of Representatives unanimously passed a measure introduced by Steven C. LaTourette recognizing Feller for his military service and the 60th anniversary of his historic 1946 season, when he went 26–15 with a then-record 348 strikeouts and a 2.18 earned-run average and led the American League in wins, shutouts, strikeouts, games pitched, and innings. In September 2006, fans voted him the Indians Hometown Hero, the player who most represents the franchise.

In March 2000, he was named an honorary member of the Green Berets, in recognition of his work for U.S. troops in Vietnam. In 1969, fans voted him the greatest living right-handed pitcher as part of baseball's centennial celebration.

Feller said he still got between 10 and 20 requests each week for appearances or interviews, and he rarely met an autograph seeker he didn't oblige. One local reporter tells a story about approaching Feller for an interview, when the most famous Indian mistook the reporter's intentions, grabbed his notebook and pen, and signed an autograph instead.

At 87, Feller makes frequent appearances on behalf of the Indians, and it's not often he turns down their requests to meet with fans or business associates. On one lovely late summer evening during the 2006 season, he was preparing to autograph a couple of dozen pictures for the communications department and then leave his seat in the press box to go down to a loge to "shake hands, smile, tell a rainy day story, and come back." Feller figures it's the least he can do.

"It goes with the territory," he said. "You have to accept that. Being in the public eye, the pluses far exceed the minuses."

Feller has been in the public eye since he signed with the Indians for $1 and an autographed ball as a raw but hard-throwing 16-year-old from Van Meter, Iowa. Indians scout Cy Slapnicka stumbled upon Feller while looking for another pitcher.

According to *The Cleveland Indians,* by Franklin Lewis, Slapnicka hurried back to Cleveland, where he told the team's board of directors, "Gentlemen, I've found the greatest young pitcher I ever saw. I suppose this sounds like the same old stuff to you, but I want you to believe me. This boy that I found out in Iowa will be the greatest pitcher the world has ever known.

"I found this boy, name of Bob Feller, in a small town not far from Des Moines—Van Meter, they call it. I know that country out there pretty well. My home section, you see. Well, my friends told me about this boy, so I went to see him pitch. I only saw him pitch once before I signed him. Went back to the Feller farm that same night and the boy's father and I made a deal."

The signing of Feller on July 25, 1935, did not come off without a hitch. At the time, baseball rules prohibited major league teams from signing sandlot players. When a minor league team in Iowa tried to sign Feller in 1935, his contract with the Indians came to light. The Iowa team complained to Judge Kenesaw Mountain Landis, the baseball commissioner. Landis could have voided Feller's contract and declared him a free agent. But Feller told Landis he wanted to stay with the Indians, so Landis fined the team $7,500, which was awarded to Iowa.

Feller, born November 3, 1918, actually was so young his father had to cosign the contract. In some ways, that was only fitting because it was his father who bought the nine-year-old Feller his first flannel uniform from a mail-order catalog, persuaded him to become a pitcher instead of a shortstop when he was 15, and built him his own ballpark on their farm 20 miles west of Des Moines, a

Bob Feller has been a fixture of Tribe lore since he signed with the Indians for $1 and an autographed ball as a raw but hard-throwing 16-year-old from Van Meter, Iowa.

That Bob Feller has his own museum back in Van Meter, Iowa?

park that served as the model for the one in the movie *Field of Dreams*. The farm had no electricity or indoor plumbing, but it was the perfect place for Robert and his sister Marguerite to grow up. His dad was a farmer. His mother was a teacher and a registered nurse, but she quit working so she could be there when her children got home from school.

After signing with the Indians, Feller, who threw five no-hitters in high school, pitched in the state high school tournament in 1936, then went to the Indians and struck out eight in three innings of an exhibition game against the St. Louis Cardinals. In his first start, on August 23, 1936, he threw a six-hitter and struck out 15 St. Louis Browns in a 4–1 victory, just missing the American League record of 16 strikeouts. In his fifth start, he threw a two-hitter and struck out 17 Philadelphia Athletics in a 5–2 victory to tie Dizzy Dean's single-game record. He finished his first season 5–3.

In all the books and stories written about Feller, there is no mention that he was ever homesick or unsure of himself, despite leaving home at the age of 17. Slapnicka and his wife, along with trainer Lefty Weisman and his family, took the young Feller under their wings, and they seemed to be enough for him.

"My mother hated that I never got homesick," Feller said, laughing. "She said, 'All those years I brought that kid up and he didn't even miss me.' But when I was a kid about nine, I read something Thomas Edison said: Find out what you want to do with your life and do it and never work again. That's what I did."

After his first season, the 6'0", 185-pound Feller (who earned the nickname "Rapid Robert" for his fastball delivery) went back home to Van Meter. Despite starting his senior year several weeks late, he was voted president of his class of 17. Then he left for spring training in February, where he was the only player with a tutor making him do his homework. All told, he had a five-month senior year. Unfortunately, early in the 1937 season he slipped while throwing a pitch in the rain and hurt his arm and was out for two months. That did allow him to return to Van Meter for his high school graduation, which was covered by NBC Radio. Think of the worldwide coverage such an event would attract these days.

He returned to the Indians, and later that season in a game against the New York Yankees, with the score tied 1–1 in the ninth inning, he threw a change-up that Joe DiMaggio knocked out of the park for a grand-slam home run in a 5–1 victory. After the game, some of the Yankees said Feller didn't belong in the majors and should be in the minors, which was the start of his rivalry with DiMaggio and the Indians' rivalry with the Yankees.

It was a good thing the Indians didn't listen to the Yankees. Feller went 9–7 in 1937. On October 2, 1938, the last day of the season, Feller struck out 18 Detroit Tigers to set the major league record for that time. He finished that season 17–11, went 24–9 in 1939, 27–11 in 1940—including the only Opening Day no-hitter in the history of major league baseball—and 25–13 in 1941.

Then the most amazing thing happened. Two days after the Japanese bombed Pearl Harbor, Bob Feller, the preeminent pitcher of his time, enlisted in the navy. As the sole support of his family back in Iowa, he would not have had to go. But he felt it was his patriotic duty to do so. He wanted no part of a stateside desk job, either. He served 44 months, most of them aboard the U.S.S. *Alabama,* earning eight battle stars as a chief gunnery officer.

"I would argue that 'Rapid Robert' Feller is a hero in every sense of the word, both on and off the field," LaTourette said in a press release accompanying the 2006 passage of the measure honoring

Great Words

Bob Feller's Recipe for a Good Life in Baseball

1. Stay in general good health.
2. Observe proper nutrition.
3. Stay off the booze.
4. Don't do drugs.
5. Get enough sleep the night before you play.
6. Exercise all year round.

IF ONLY . . . The 1954 World Series had started in Cleveland, Feller thinks the outcome would have been different. He doesn't think Bob Lemon would have lost the opener at home, and he says Vic Wertz's fly ball that Willie Mays caught over his shoulder would have been a game-winning home run. Furthermore, Feller says, Dusty Rhodes's game-winning home run would not have been a home run in cavernous Cleveland Municipal Stadium. If the Indians had won the first game, the whole tone of the Series might have been different. Clearly, the Indians would not have been swept by the Giants.

Feller. "He remains completely devoted to his sport, to the Indians, and to our men and women in uniform. He is a wonderful and self-less American."

Added Representative Dennis Kucinich in the press release, "Bob Feller epitomized everything we hoped our professional athletes could ever be."

Feller missed nearly four full seasons, pitching in just a handful of games at the end of the 1945 season. In his first game back, on August 24, 1945, a crowd of 46,477 watched Feller strike out 12 Tigers in a 4–2 victory over rival Hal Newhouser. He finished that season 5–3, setting the stage for his incredible performance in 1946.

Some estimate that Feller would have had 100 or more victories had he not enlisted, but Feller could not care less.

"I made a lot of mistakes in my life," he said. "Joining the navy two days after Pearl Harbor was not one of them."

Thanks to the talents of Feller and his teammates, the Indians became one of the dominant teams in baseball, winning the World Series in 1948 and returning in 1954, only to be swept by the New York Giants. Feller, though, never was able to win a World Series game. In 1948, a controversial call by umpire Bill Stewart allowed pinch runner Phil Masi to score the game's only run in the eighth inning of Game 1 against the Boston Braves. Feller, who pitched a two-hitter, and Lou Boudreau thought they had picked off Masi at second base, and photos indicated they had. But Stewart called Masi safe. In later years, Masi admitted he was out, and Stewart admitted he made a mistake. Feller also lost Game 5, 11–5. Though Feller had a 13–3 record in the regular season, Manager Al Lopez didn't call on him to pitch in the 1954 World Series. Feller said he was never told why, and he never asked.

Feller, who was instrumental in the creation of the Baseball Players Association and the pension plan, retired after the 1956 season, and his career has been unmatched. He fin-

TRIVIA

What was the name of the ballpark Bob Feller's father built on their Iowa farm?

Answers to the trivia questions are on pages 167–168.

ished with a 266–162 record, 3.25 ERA, and .621 winning percentage. He had three no-hitters and 12 one-hitters. He led the league in wins six times and in strikeouts seven times. He threw a fastball 104 mph, faster than a speeding motorcycle, during a promotional stunt in Chicago's Lincoln Park in 1940, and hit 107.9 at the Aberdeen Ordinance Plant in Washington, D.C., the fastest pitch ever measured with a speed-measuring device. He was inducted into the Hall of Fame in 1962 on the first ballot, and he was the first player to have his number (19) retired by the Indians in 1957. The only reason he never won a Cy Young Award was that it wasn't established until the year he retired. Feller, who named the late Jim Hegan as the best catcher he ever had, still leads the Indians in innings pitched (3,827), wins (266), strikeouts (2,581), complete games (279), games started (484), and All-Star appearances (eight, including starts in 1941 and 1946). He won 20 or more games six times, including a career high 27 in 1940. He was the Major League Player of the Year in 1940 and was voted the Indians' Man of the Year in 1951.

In addition to retiring his number, the Indians honored Feller by placing a 10-foot-tall bronze statue of him at the East Ninth Street entrance to Jacobs Field.

"It's nice to be immortalized when you're still alive," Feller said.

The best news for the Indians and baseball? Feller has a 16-year-old grandson Daniel who is showing some signs of being a good American League pitcher in the Hartford area.

Lou Boudreau: The Boy Manager

Lou Boudreau always got ahead of himself.

His high school basketball team was the state champion when he was a sophomore—and he was the captain on that team, as well as the teams that made it to the state finals his junior and senior years.

He also was the captain of the University of Illinois basketball team as a junior.

And by the time he was 24, he was coaching the freshman basketball team at Illinois that would go on to be known as the "Whiz Kids."

So why wouldn't he think he was ready to manage the Cleveland Indians?

He'd been playing in Cleveland since 1939. He even played one game there in 1938. In his first full season in Cleveland in 1940, he hit .295 with 101 RBIs and was named to the All-Star team. That had been an odd year. The players rebelled against Manager Oscar Vitt, earning the nickname "the Crybabies."

Vitt had been fired after the season and replaced by Roger Peckinpaugh. But when former superscout C.C. "Cy" Slapnicka resigned as general manager after the 1941 season, Peckinpaugh was promoted, which left the Indians looking for a manager.

Boudreau sent in his résumé. But he was as surprised as anyone when the Indians called and wanted to schedule an interview with the board of directors. He told them he was a physical education major and had always planned to go into coaching. He told them he thought he could handle the players and the press.

Apparently, he was not very convincing. In the first vote of the directors after the interview, they voted 11–1 not to hire him. But that one vote belonged to George Martin, chairman of the board of the Cleveland-based Sherwin Williams. Eventually, Martin convinced the others that Boudreau was their man, and during a rare night press conference on November 25, 1941, Boudreau was introduced as the Indians' new manager.

"The more I inspected the qualifications of various other candidates, the more I became convinced that we couldn't afford not to take advantage of Lou Boudreau's natural gift of leadership," owner Alva Bradley told the reporters. "I didn't know of another man of whom I could be so certain that he would be thoroughly respected by the players, press, and public. Lou is smart, he's a great ball

Lou Boudreau poses with his wife before Game 1 of the 1948 World Series against the Boston Braves.

TRIVIA

Besides baseball and basketball, what other sport did Boudreau attempt to play at the University of Illinois?

Answers to the trivia questions are on pages 167–168.

player, a fine young man, a fighter, and a leader."

The reporters were somewhat surprised, but not completely.

In his book *The Cleveland Indians,* Franklin Lewis wrote, "From that first minute he wore a Cleveland uniform, in August of 1939, Lou Boudreau was the key man in the field. He was a magnet drawing to him all the responsibilities and requests for judgment usually reserved for gray managers sitting in the shade of the dugout."

Of course, not everyone shared in the excitement. According to Lewis, one Detroit reporter wrote, "Being made manager of that outfit after two years in the majors and having to face the irascible Cleveland public and a press box full of second guessers is enough to warrant calling out the Society for the Prevention of Cruelty to Children."

Looking back, Boudreau did try some childish stuff. His request that the reporters show him their stories before they sent them in fell on deaf ears. And when he posted rah-rah signs around the locker room for his first spring training in 1942, he found the signs ripped down and stained with tobacco juice. He knew players were calling him "Joe College" behind his back.

But he was trying to rally a team that had lost a number of its best players, including pitcher Bob Feller, to World War II. (Boudreau was excused from the draft because of his chronically troublesome ankles.)

As a manager that first year, Boudreau made a better shortstop. The Indians finished 75–79–2, but he hit .283 and made the All-Star team for the third time.

"The season was a learning year for me," Boudreau admitted in his autobiography. "It also was a challenge."

But Boudreau had faced many challenges in his life. Born July 17, 1917, in Harvey, Illinois, Boudreau was a good playmaker and passer on the basketball team at Thornton Township High School, which didn't have a baseball team. His dad, Louis Boudreau Sr., was a machinist who had played semipro and minor league baseball. His parents divorced when he was seven, and his mother remarried a shoemaker who was not a sports fan.

Boudreau earned a basketball scholarship to the University of Illinois, where he also played third base on the baseball team. He was discovered by Indians scout Harold Irelan but didn't want to sign a contract and jeopardize his college eligibility. Irelan said that was no problem, as long as he promised he'd sign with Cleveland when his eligibility was up. To sweeten the pot, Irelan promised the Boudreau family $1,000—$500 for his mother and stepfather, $500 for his dad. Unfortunately, because the stepfather was upset he had to share the money, he informed Big Ten commissioner John L. Griffith of the deal, and Boudreau lost his senior year of eligibility in basketball and baseball.

He signed to play with the Caesar's All-Americans of Hammond, Indiana, in the National Basketball League, the forerunner of the National Basketball Association. In 1938 he played for the Indians farm team in Cedar Rapids, but was called up for one game, going 0-for-1 with a walk.

In 1939 he was promoted to Buffalo, where he was moved to shortstop since the Indians had All-Star Ken Keltner at third base. He was called up on August 7, 1939, and never left.

"From the moment he trotted out to shortstop for infield practice, Boudreau had the crowd in the palm of a right hand that was to become world famous," Lewis wrote. "He had the movements of the natural athlete. He was graceful and commanding."

Under his commanding presence, the Indians improved to 82–71 in 1943. Boudreau batted .286, made the All-Star team again, and led the American League shortstops in fielding percentage. In 1944 the team's record dipped to 72–82–1, but Boudreau won the batting title with a .327 average and set a record for shortstops with a .978 fielding percentage. He also took part in 134 double plays, the most for a shortstop at the time.

Feller returned late in the 1945 season, but the Indians still were just 73–72–2. They were plugging along at 26–32 in 1946, when Bill Veeck bought the team.

Veeck loved publicity and liked to shake things up. He wanted people to have fun at the ballpark, but it wasn't always fun for those who worked for him. Especially his manager.

"Veeck was like a whirlwind once he got situated in Cleveland," Boudreau wrote in his book. "We always had three teams—one on the field, another coming, and one going. We never had the same team on the field for more than a week at a time."

Veeck, who threw a special night in honor of "the Greatest Shortstop Ever Left Off the All-Star Team" when Boudreau did not make the 1946 All-Star team, was not high on his great shortstop's managing skills. He thought about replacing Boudreau as manager with Jimmy Dykes, but he couldn't afford to lose the services of one of the best shortstops in the game.

In his autobiography, *Veeck—As in Wreck,* Veeck wrote, "I liked Louie. I still like Louie.... My main objection to Lou was that he managed by hunch and desperation. You ask Casey Stengel why he made a certain move and he will tell you about a roommate he had in 1919 who had demonstrated some principle Casey was now putting into effect. You ask Lou and he will say, 'The way we were going, we had to do something.' If there is a better formula for making a bad situation worse, I have never heard of it."

Of course, Veeck had to hand it to Boudreau when he devised an ingenious way to stop—at least temporarily—the great Ted Williams. The Indians were in Boston for a doubleheader on July 14, 1946. Boudreau set a record with five extra-base hits in a game (four doubles and a home run), but the Indians lost the opener 11–10, as Williams hit three home runs and drove in eight.

IF ONLY . . . Indians general manager Hank Greenberg had not fired the 33-year-old Lou Boudreau as manager after the 1950 season, the outcome of the 1954 World Series might have been different. Although Boudreau never again enjoyed the managerial success he had in Cleveland, he seemed to make the right moves when it counted most with the Indians and was just coming into his prime when he was released.

Boudreau was steaming, and in between games he vowed to do something about it. Statistics showed that 95 percent of Williams's hits went to right field. So Boudreau devised a shift—sometimes called the Williams shift and sometimes referred to as the Boudreau shift—and had his first baseman and right fielder hug the right-field line. The second baseman moved closer to first and back on the grass. Boudreau played shortstop to the right of second base, and the third baseman played behind second on the edge of the grass. The center fielder moved toward right field, while the left fielder was to cover everything else in the outfield. Williams grounded out and walked twice, although the Indians still lost, 6–4.

The Indians finished the 1946 season with a 68–86–2 record. Most years that would have prompted Veeck to make a move for 1947, but he didn't. At least not a managerial one. Instead, he made a ground-breaking move, signing Larry Doby as the first African American in the American League, just three months after Jackie Robinson broke the color barrier in the National League.

In his autobiography, Boudreau said he did not know Doby was coming, and he was skeptical at first, thinking it was another one of Veeck's publicity stunts.

According to Thomas Joseph Moore's biography of Doby, when Doby joined the team, Boudreau issued a statement that read, "The acquisition of Larry Doby, an infielder formerly with the Newark Eagles team, is a routine baseball purchase in my mind. Creed, race, or color are not factors in baseball success, whether it be in the major or minor leagues. Ability and character are the only factors. Doby will be given every chance, as will any other deserving recruit, to prove that he has the ability to make good with us. The reports we have received on his ability are outstanding. I hope that he can succeed with us as he has with other teams."

Though Doby struggled that first year, the Indians improved to 80–74–3. But that didn't stop Veeck from trying to trade Boudreau, whose contract had expired. Veeck had never liked the idea of the "Boy Manager," and he was worried about Boudreau's chronically sore ankles. So when the St. Louis Browns called offering shortstop Vern Stephens, Veeck surveyed the Cleveland writers—off the record, of course. Veeck later admitted that at one point the deal was so close, he had Al Lopez standing by waiting to be introduced as new manager. But when a line about the proposed trade appeared in the Chicago papers, the news exploded all over Cleveland. Fans went crazy, beseeching Veeck not to go through with the deal. In his autobiography, Veeck insisted he got a telegram from a Cleveland minister that read, "If Boudreau doesn't return to Cleveland, don't you bother to return either."

Veeck made a great show of working the streets and bars and restaurants in Cleveland, listening to the fans. Veeck took credit for changing his mind in reaction to the fans' outburst, when in actuality the Browns had already withdrawn the deal.

Naturally, Boudreau refused Veeck's new one-year deal, and naturally Veeck had to give him two.

It all paid off in the magical year of 1948, when everything went right.

The Indians finished 97–58–1, and Boudreau hit .355 with 18 homers and 106 RBIs and was the league's MVP. Still, Cleveland finished tied with the Red Sox. In the one-game American League playoff, Boudreau opted to start rookie Gene Bearden, a left-handed knuckleball pitcher, on one day's rest. Just to make sure that worked out, Boudreau hit two home runs in the Indians' 8–3 victory.

After the game, Boudreau received a telegram from Emma Regina Martin, widow of George Martin, who had convinced the Indians to hire Boudreau in 1942.

"Mr. Martin would have been proud of his boys and their manager," it read.

The Indians won the best-of-seven World Series against the Boston Braves, four games to two, and Boudreau batted .273 for the six games.

TOP 10

Indians Managers (by Victories)

1.	Lou Boudreau	728
2.	Mike Hargrove	721
3.	Tris Speaker	617
4.	Al Lopez	570
5.	Roger Peckinpaugh	490
6.	Nap Lajoie	377
7.	Lee Fohl	327
8.	Pat Corrales	280
9.	Birdie Tebbetts	278
10.	Alvin Dark	266

Unfortunately, the Indians could not recapture that magic in 1949 or 1950, and on November 10, 1950, Indians general manager Hank Greenberg fired Boudreau, in spite of a 728–649 (.529) record in nine years, still the most wins for a Cleveland manager.

Boudreau signed with the Red Sox in 1951 and became their manager from 1952 to 1954. Then he managed in Kansas City from 1954 to 1956. He joined the Chicago Cubs as a broadcaster in 1958, but on May 4, 1960, he replaced Charley Grimm as manager. When the Cubs finished 54–83 under Boudreau, he returned to the broadcast booth for the next 30 years. His managerial record stands at 1,162–1,224 (.487).

The eight-time All-Star, who also managed the AL to an 11–7 victory over the NL in the 1949 All-Star Game, finished his career with a .295 average in 1,646 games and was elected to the Hall of Fame in 1970, getting 232 out of a possible 300 votes from writers.

Upon his induction, Commissioner Bowie Kuhn said of Boudreau, "The most remarkable thing about this remarkable man was the way he stretched the wonderful skills he had into superlative skills. As a shortstop he was a human computer, he knew all the hitters' habits, he knew all the moves of the base runners, he knew what the pitcher was going to pitch, he had an instinct for where the ball would be hit, and from all of this he fashioned the wonderful ballplayer that we knew as Lou Boudreau in the major leagues."

Boudreau, whose No. 5 was retired by the Indians in 1970, died on August 10, 2001, at St. James Hospital in Olympia Fields, Illinois. He was 84.

In a column the day after Boudreau's death, Bill Livingston of *The* (Cleveland) *Plain Dealer* asked: "Was Boudreau a better player or manager in 1948? Was Michelangelo a better painter or sculptor?"

Larry Doby
Makes History

The photograph is a famous one. It has been printed and reprinted hundreds of times. In the black-and-white shot, pitcher Steve Gromek, his hair mussed and sweaty, is on the left, with his arms wrapped around the neck of Larry Doby, who is wearing an Indians cap pushed slightly back on his head by the enthusiasm of the hug. The two are cheek to cheek, and their matching smiles are so wide their eyes are nearly crinkled shut.

The moment of celebration was captured on October 9, 1948, after Doby's home run gave Gromek and the Indians a 2–1 victory over the Boston Braves and a three-games-to-one lead in the best-of-seven 1948 World Series.

Over the years, similar photographs have become commonplace, whether it's the quarterback hugging the running back who just scored the winning touchdown in the Super Bowl, or the center and point guard celebrating a winning basket in the NBA Finals. No one takes a second look now.

But in 1948 that was not the case. Baseball had been integrated only since the beginning of the 1947 season. Gromek was white. Doby was black. That photo is believed to be the first widely circulated picture showing how sports could bring the races together. In its own way, it is as memorable as Alfred Eisenstaedt's V-J Day photo of the sailor kissing the nurse in Times Square on August 14, 1945.

In fact, when Cleveland *Plain Dealer* sportswriter Bob Dolgan interviewed Doby in 1998 for a story that was part of a series the paper did to commemorate the 50th anniversary of the Indians' last

6—Number of retired Indians numbers. The Indians retired Doby's No. 14 on July 3, 1994, the 47th anniversary of his debut in Cleveland. He is one of six Indians to receive that honor. The others are No. 3 Earl Averill, No. 5 Lou Boudreau, No. 18 Mel Harder, No. 19 Bob Feller, and No. 21 Bob Lemon.

World Series title, he asked Doby his personal highlight of the season and Doby replied, "Gromek."

"It was an emotional time," Doby told Dolgan for the story, which became part of Dolgan's collection of articles featured in his book *Heroes, Scamps, and Good Guys.*

"We had won and we showed respect for each other. The picture showed that black and white people could get along and work together. I don't think too many people were ready for that type of picture in '48."

Gromek, also interviewed for the series, told Dolgan, "Color was never an issue with me. Doby won the game for me. I was happy. I always got along well with him. He won a lot of games for me with his bat and glove."

An 11-year-old Wayne Embry, growing up in Springfield, Ohio, also took note of the photograph. He had not been an Indians fan, but became one when Doby joined the team.

"I remember when Larry Doby came up," said Embry, who became the first African American general manager in sports when the Milwaukee Bucks named him to that post in 1972. "Certain things you never forget. When breakthroughs occurred, they were significant."

His reaction to seeing that famous photograph back in 1948?

Said Embry, "I remember thinking, 'Wow. Maybe there is hope for us.'"

For Doby, the first African American to play in the American League, it was a long road to that 1948 World Series title.

It started in the poor Black Bottom section of Camden, South Carolina, where Doby was born on December 13, 1923. His father, David, was a stable hand who split his time between Camden and Saratoga. His mother, Etta, eventually split from his father and sought work as a domestic in Paterson, New Jersey, leaving young Lawrence, nicknamed Bubba, with her mother, Augusta Brooks.

Doby was raised by his grandmother and later moved in with his aunt and uncle, Alice and James Cookie, and their five children. His father drowned when Doby was 11.

Doby started at the public Jackson School, but his aunt and uncle switched him to the Methodist Browning School–Mather Academy in Camden. More important, he learned to play baseball under Richard DuBose, who remembered David Doby as a first baseman who was a good hitter.

After Doby graduated from eighth grade, his mother insisted he attended Eastside High School in Paterson. It was an integrated school, if 25 African Americans in a school population of 1,200 counts as integrated, with a good academic reputation. There, Doby met the woman who would become his wife, Helyn Curvy, and earned 11 varsity letters in football, basketball, baseball, and track. He thought

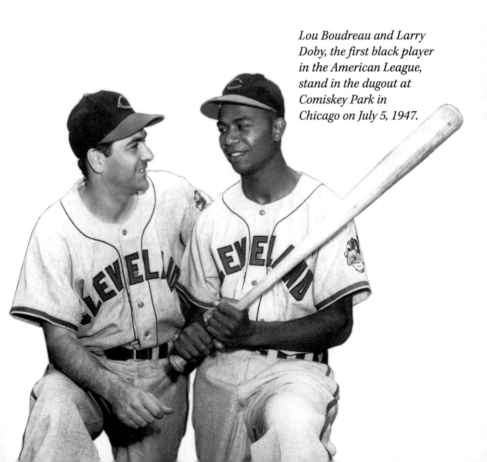

Lou Boudreau and Larry Doby, the first black player in the American League, stand in the dugout at Comiskey Park in Chicago on July 5, 1947.

he'd like to become a physical education teacher and coach. In his spare time, he played semipro baseball and recreational basketball, even joining the Harlem Renaissance pro team that won the National Basketball Tournament in 1938, according to author Joseph Thomas Moore's fine biography of Doby, *Pride against Prejudice*. Even before he graduated from high school in 1942, Doby, using the alias Larry Walker, played for the Newark Eagles in the Negro Leagues.

He planned to attend Long Island University and play basketball for Clair Bee. But with America's entry into World War II, Doby decided to attend Virginia Union, which had an ROTC program. After he helped Virginia Union win its conference championship, he was drafted, wound up in the navy, and was sent to the Pacific atoll Ulithi. It was there he learned of Branch Rickey's decision to sign Jackie Robinson.

After an honorable discharge in 1946, Doby returned to the Eagles and married Helyn on August 10 of that year. It ended up being quite a year for the 22-year-old Doby, as the Eagles won the Negro World Series.

Not long after, Cleveland owner Bill Veeck began an active campaign to sign a black player to integrate the American League as Jackie Robinson had done in the National League at the start of the 1947 season.

"I have always had a strong feeling for minority groups," Veeck wrote in his autobiography, *Veeck—As in Wreck* with Ed Linn. "The pat curbstone explanation would be that having lost a leg myself, I can very easily identify myself with the deprived. Right? Wrong. I had tried to buy the Philadelphia Phillies and stock it with Negro players well before I went into the service.... My only personal experience with discrimination is that I am a left-hander in a right-handed world, a subject on which I can become violent.

"Thinking about it, it seems to me that all my life I have been fighting against the status quo, against the tyranny of the fossilized majority rule. I would suppose that whatever impels me to battle the old fossils of baseball also draws me to the side of the underdog. I would prefer to think of it as an essential decency."

First Veeck hired an African American public relations man, Lou Jones, to research the Negro Leagues and also to serve as a companion for the player who would join the Indians. That player, of course, was Doby. Veeck paid the Eagles $10,000 to buy Doby's contract, though he turned down the offer of eventual Hall of Famer Monte Irvin for another $1,000. The Indians announced the deal on July 3, 1947.

The deal started a friendship that lasted until Veeck's death in 1986.

"He was one of the greatest people I ever met," Doby said of Veeck. "I lost my father...and I certainly would have liked him to be the same kind of man Bill Veeck was.... We remained friends until the day he died. He personified the phrase, 'human being.'"

Doby joined the Indians in Chicago, where the 23-year-old second baseman who was batting more than .400 for the Eagles signed his contract on July 5, 1947, three months after Robinson broke the color barrier in baseball. Though there was no story on the front page, the Cleveland *Plain Dealer* sports section featured two photos and a couple of stories, including one in which writer Gordon Cobbledick referred to the 6'1", 180-pound Doby as "the coppery-skinned colored boy" and later said Doby made a pleasing appearance in street clothes. In a later column, Cobbledick wrote, "People are doing a lot of unnecessary guessing as to how Larry Doby, the Indians newest rookie, will be accepted by his teammates and by the customers. He will be accepted by both groups if he proves to be a good ballplayer and a good human being, and will be rejected by both if the opposite is true. How do I know? Well, the Cleveland Browns of the All-America Football Conference signed two Negro players last year to the deep consternation of their rival teams. There had been no colored boys in the white professional league, and it was evident that all except the Browns intended to keep it that way if possible. Today, something less than a year later, every team in the All-America Conference is beating the bushes in a desperate effort to find a good Negro football player or two—another Bill Willis or another Marion Motley."

IF ONLY . . . Bill Veeck had bought the Indians before 1946, Larry Doby might have been the first African American player in baseball. Veeck was committed to integration, and if he'd gotten a slightly earlier start, Doby might have beaten Jackie Robinson to the major leagues, or at least started the 1947 season with him.

After signing, Doby went to meet Manager Lou Boudreau, who introduced him to the other players in the clubhouse. Two reportedly refused to shake Doby's hand—Les Fleming and Eddie Robinson. Robinson also reportedly refused to lend Doby a first baseman's mitt, though Robinson later insisted it was less about race and more about being worried about his spot on the team.

Then Boudreau and Doby walked to the field and began to play catch as an ovation greeted Doby's arrival. Doby made one appearance as a pinch-hitter in the seventh inning but struck out. He returned to the end of the bench and put his head in his hands. A popular tale had teammate Joe Gordon striking out next and then taking a seat next to Doby and putting his head in his hands, too. But according to biographer Moore and *Plain Dealer* reports the next day, Gordon walked to open the inning and was on third base when Doby struck out.

At any rate, the significance of Doby's appearance was not lost on Cleveland Jackson, a writer for the *Call and Post* newspaper, who wrote on July 12, 1947, "For Larry Doby, it took but a few short minutes to walk up to that plate. But for 13 million American Negroes, that simple action was the successful climax of a long uphill fight whose annals are like the saga of the [black] race."

The rest of the weekend passed fairly uneventfully, although Doby, who played at first base in the second game of a doubleheader on Sunday, had to stay in a different hotel than the rest of the team, which was staying in a downtown, "whites only" hotel.

When Doby arrived in Cleveland on Tuesday, July 8, he was greeted at the train station by Willis and Motley, the two Browns who had integrated the All-America Football Conference. In an interview that ran in the *Plain Dealer* that day, Doby said, "When I first went to bat in Chicago, I was so scared I didn't even know how many men were out, and all I had to do was look at the scoreboard. I never did swing at a strike, I was so tense at the plate. It all seems like a dream now."

Despite the support of Veeck and the friendship of players like Gordon and Jim Hegan, the adjustment to the American League was a tough one for Doby, who batted just .156 (5-of-32) his first season, when he suffered many indignities from rival fans and others, including the hoteliers and restaurateurs who refused to serve him.

"It was one of the toughest things I ever had to go through," he told Dolgan in 2001.

After the season, Coach Bill McKechnie told Doby he was unlikely to unseat Gordon at second base and suggested he read a book to learn how to play the outfield. Doby picked up a copy of *How to Play the Outfield* by Tommy Henrich of the New York Yankees. The book and some tips from former Indians star player and manager Tris Speaker during spring training allowed Doby to make the team as a right fielder in 1948. When Thurman Tucker was injured, Doby moved to center field and stayed eight years, earning many accolades. He helped the Indians win the 1948 World Series and was the Indians' Man of the Year in 1950, when he batted a career-high .326. He led the AL with 32 home runs in 1952 and led the league in homers (32) and RBIs (126) as the Indians won the AL pennant in 1954 before being swept by the New York Giants in the World Series.

The Indians traded him to the Chicago White Sox for shortstop Chico Carrasquel and center fielder Jim Busby on October 25, 1955, but got him back from Baltimore in a trade on April 1, 1958. On May 13, 1959, Cleveland sent him to Detroit for Tito Francona. The Indians retired his No. 14 on July 3, 1994.

In his major league career, Doby batted .283 with 253 home runs. He appeared in seven All-Star Games.

"I'm happy with the career I had," he said.

TRIVIA

According to the Baseball Hall of Fame, in 1962 two players became the first former major leaguers to play for a professional Japanese team, the Chunichi Dragons. Doby was one of them. Who was the other?

Answers to the trivia questions are on pages 167–168.

By the NUMBERS

27—Number of players enshrined in the Baseball Hall of Fame who played for or managed the Indians. This total does not include former general manager Bill Evans, who was inducted in 1973; former owner Bill Veeck, inducted in 1991; or former general manager Hank Greenberg, inducted in 1956.

Name	Year Enshrined
Walter Johnson	1936
Nap Lajoie	1937
Tris Speaker	1937
Cy Young	1937
Bob Feller	1962
Elmer Flick	1963
Sam Rice	1963
Stanley Coveleski	1969
Lou Boudreau	1970
Satchel Paige	1971
Early Wynn	1972
Earl Averill	1975
Ralph Kiner	1975
Bob Lemon	1976
Joe Sewell	1977
Al Lopez	1977
Addie Joss	1978
Frank Robinson	1982
Hoyt Wilhelm	1985
Gaylord Perry	1991
Hal Newhouser	1992
Steve Carlton	1994
Phil Niekro	1997
Larry Doby	1998
Dave Winfield	2001
Eddie Murray	2003
Dennis Eckersley	2004

He did not seem bitter about any of the poor treatment he received.

"Life is too short for that," he once said. "People who judge others based on the color of their skin have more problems than I do."

After retiring in 1959, Doby played in Japan, then became a scout and batting coach for Montreal and a first-base coach for the Indians. He became the second African American manager (after Cleveland's Frank Robinson) when he took over Veeck's Chicago White Sox from former Indians teammate Bob Lemon in 1978. He later worked for the New Jersey Nets, for Major League Properties, and as an assistant to American League president Gene Budig.

When he was inducted into the Hall of Fame in 1998, 36 years after Robinson, Doby gave a short speech, thanking the people of Cleveland for treating him and his family with respect.

Five years after his induction, Doby died of cancer on June 18, 2003. He was 79.

Upon hearing of Doby's death, Indians owner Larry Dolan told *The Plain Dealer*, "He was a keystone to the history of this franchise. Now he's gone and that's a big loss.... Larry Doby was such an exciting ballplayer. We want our young players to be just like him."

At the time of Doby's death, former teammate Bob Feller told MLB.com, "He was a great American, he served the country in World War II, and was a great ball player. He was kind of like Buzz Aldrin, the second man on the moon, because he was the second African American player in the majors."

1948: Champions at Last

It was all about Boston for the Indians in 1948.

When Cleveland lost to Detroit, 7–1, and Boston beat New York, 10–5, on the last day of the season, the Indians and the Red Sox finished atop the American League with identical 97–58–1 records, forcing the first AL championship playoff game, and only the second in major league history.

The next day, October 4, Ken Keltner hit a three-run home run in the fourth inning and rookie left-hander Gene Bearden pitched a five-hitter on one day's rest to lift the Indians to an 8–3 victory that clinched the AL pennant. Lou Boudreau went 4-for-4 with two home runs to help the Indians advance to the World Series for the first time since 1920. Their opponent? The Boston Braves.

Game 1, Wednesday, October 6. At Boston 1, Cleveland 0— Bob Feller actually outpitched Johnny Sain, allowing just two hits to Sain's four, but a controversial umpire's call in the eighth inning allowed pinch runner Phil Masi to score the game's only run.

"It was a tough one for Feller to lose and a great game for Sain to win, but that's always the way," Boston manager Billy Southworth told reporters after the game.

Feller walked catcher Bill Salkeld to lead off the inning. Phil Masi ran for him and went to second on a sacrifice. Eddie Stanky was intentionally walked to set up the double play. Feller threw to Boudreau to try to pick off Masi, but umpire Bill Stewart called Masi safe, although photos seemed to indicate Masi was out. Feller got Sain to fly out, but Tommy Holmes singled to drive in Masi.

"I'm sure that Masi was out," Boudreau told reporters after the game. "Stewart is a National League umpire, and he is not

Relief pitcher Gene Bearden (center) embraces starting pitcher Bob Lemon (left) and catcher Jim Hegan as they celebrate in the dressing room after winning the World Series in Boston on October 11, 1948.

acquainted with our pickoff play. I don't think he was in a good position to see the tag. I know I got him."

According to author Russ Schneider in the third edition of *The Cleveland Indians Encyclopedia*, Masi told Feller years later that Boudreau had, in fact, tagged him out. Masi also told Feller that Stewart had admitted to him in private that he'd made a mistake.

Game 2, Thursday, October 7. Cleveland 4, at Boston 1— Player/manager Lou Boudreau and center fielder Larry Doby each had a double and an RBI, and Bob Lemon sprinkled eight hits over nine innings as the Indians rebounded with a 4–1 victory to tie the Series. Ironically, Lemon's throw to Boudreau picked off Earl Torgeson on the same pickoff play in the first inning.

"Still no prediction on how long it's going to last," Boudreau told reporters after the game. "Just going along as we have all season— out to win the game coming up."

Said Lemon to reporters after the game, "The toughest thing for me the last few days has been sitting on the bench with the pennant at stake. That would give a guy ulcers a lot faster than pitching. Sure, there were a few butterflies in my stomach when I walked out there for the first inning, but they disappeared with the first pitch."

Game 3, Friday, October 8. At Cleveland 2, Boston 0—Left-handed knuckleballer Gene Bearden almost beat the Braves by himself. The former first baseman allowed just five hits and had two of the Indians' five hits, including a double, as Cleveland took a 2–1 lead in the Series.

"Always wanted Gene to be a pitcher, but it took a lot of per-suading," Bearden's father, Henry, told reporters after the game. "Finally got him off first base and on to the mound, but he still likes hitting just about as well as pitching. Didn't look bad with the stick today, either."

Said Southworth to reporters, "We'll be back with Johnny Sain to even it up. This won't get the boys down. They don't lose that easily."

Game 4, Saturday, October 9. At Cleveland 2, Boston 1—The Indians jumped on Sain for a run in the first inning, and Doby hit a 410-foot home run in the third. Steve Gromek's seven-hitter allowed that lead to stand up and the Indians moved a game from their second World Series title. Marv Rickert's seventh-inning home run was all the Braves could muster.

"I didn't sleep much last night," Gromek told reporters after the game. "I still was nervous taking my warm-up pitches. But when the first batter flied out, it was just another game until the ninth.... When I was out there for the ninth, I was thinking about this being the series and my biggest chance as a pitcher, and I believe I threw the ball faster than ever before."

IF ONLY . . . Umpire Bill Stewart had made the right call to begin with, or corrected himself when he called Phil Masi safe on a first-inning pickoff play, Bob Feller, the Indians' greatest pitcher, would have achieved the goal he set for himself—a World Series victory, which he so richly deserved.

By the NUMBERS

$6,772.07—Winning playoff share for each Indian in 1948. Each Brave got a $4,570.73 losing playoff share.

Stewart, the umpire who made the controversial safe call on Masi in the first game, was escorted off the field by several police officers after Game 4. He had called Boudreau out at third after Boudreau tried to stretch a double into a triple. Stewart also called Alvin Dark safe at a close play at first base in Game 2.

Game 5, Sunday, October 10. Boston 11, at Cleveland 5—Boston third baseman Bob Elliott hit two home runs as the Braves pummeled the Indians for 12 hits before a disappointed World Series–record crowd of 86,288. Every player in the Braves lineup had at least one hit, including starting pitcher Nels Potter. Boston took a 3–0 lead in the first, but the Indians actually held a 5–4 lead after the fourth. But the Braves added one run in the sixth and settled things once and for all with six runs in the top of the seventh, making a winner out of Warren Spahn.

"What a relief to get some runs—and pitching, too," Southworth told reporters after the game. "Gosh, we really exploded. Yep, we're right back in this series."

Game 6, Monday, October 11. Cleveland 4, at Boston 3—The Indians built a 4–1 lead in the eighth inning, but Boston kept things close with two runs in the their half of the eighth. Lemon won his second game of the series, with relief help by Bearden, who pitched his way out of a one-out, two-on jam in the eighth inning.

"Oh, I was tired," Lemon told reporters after the game. "Lou did right in taking me out. We won, though. That's all I care about."

First baseman Eddie Robinson paced the Indians offense with two hits and an RBI. Joe Gordon hit a solo home run in the sixth. It was quite a week for Bearden, who won the game that clinched a tie for the pennant, won the game that clinched the pennant, won one World Series game, and saved another as the Indians won the World Series for the first time in 28 years.

"It was Bearden's series all the way, all his," Boudreau told reporters after the game. "Gene was the key to our success."

No Sweeter Guy Than Bob Lemon

It's a good thing that Bob Lemon didn't become a pitcher until the middle of the 1946 season. Otherwise, he might not have made that nice catch in the outfield that helped save Bob Feller's no-hitter on April 30, 1946, at New York.

By that time in his career, the Indians were struggling to find a spot for the light-hitting Lemon. Born on September 22, 1920, in San Bernardino, California, Lemon grew up in Long Beach and signed with the Indians as a third baseman in 1938. He hit .309 at New Orleans in 1939 and .301 at Wilkes-Barre in 1941.

But when the Indians called him up for five games in 1941 and five more in 1942, he went 1-for-9. Given that the Indians already had All-Star Ken Keltner at third base, there was no way a guy with that anemic a batting average was going to challenge him.

A two-year stint in the navy from 1943 to 1945 during World War II interrupted Lemon's baseball career, and when he came back, the first thing Manager Lou Boudreau tried was to convert Lemon to an outfielder. But he was hitting just .180 in the middle of the 1946 season. The story goes that Lemon was headed for the Indians farm team in Baltimore until a game against Boston in the middle of that season. Boston catcher Birdie Tebbetts, who would become manager of the Indians in 1963, mentioned to Boudreau that he had batted against Lemon while they were in the service. Tebbetts told Boudreau that Lemon was a decent pitcher. Boudreau had seen Lemon pitch batting practice, so he decided to see if Lemon had what it took to pitch in a game.

TOP 10

Indians Pitchers (by Wins)

1.	Bob Feller	266
2.	Mel Harder	223
3.	Bob Lemon	207
4.	Stan Coveleski	172
5.	Early Wynn	164
6.	Addie Joss	160
7.	Willis Hudlin	157
8.	George Uhle	147
9.	Mike Garcia	142
10.	Charles Nagy	129

The 25-year-old right-hander started slowly as a reliever. He was just 4–5 with a 2.49 earned-run average the rest of 1946. But he went 11–5 with a 3.44 ERA in 1947 and he was off and running.

"He made the change so easy," Mel Harder, the former star pitcher who became the Indians' longtime pitching coach, told Bob Dolgan of *The* (Cleveland) *Plain Dealer*. "He was such a good player that everything he did was right."

His trademark pitch was his sinkerbal,l and starting in 1948, when he went 20–14 with a 2.82 earned-run average and led the league with 20 complete games and 293⅔ innings pitched, he had seven seasons with 20 victories—a team record. He even won two games to help the Indians beat the Boston Braves in the 1948 World Series, which every long-suffering Indians fan knows was the last time the team ended a season victoriously.

He beat the Braves 4–1 in the second game and came back to win the deciding sixth game, 4–3, with relief help from Gene Bearden. Though he normally stood 6' and weighed 180 pounds, he was so nervous during the playoffs that he lost 30 pounds and weighed less than 150 by the end of the World Series.

He was more than strong enough, though. Lemon became part of the Indians pitching staff known as "the Big Four." Lemon, Mike

Garcia, Bob Feller, and Early Wynn won 79 games in 1951. Lemon, Garcia, Wynn, and Art Houtteman won 80 games in 1954, when the Indians had what is generally recognized as the best pitching staff in the history of the game.

He was an All-Star seven times, was *The Sporting News*'s Pitcher of the Year in 1948, 1950, and 1954, and was the Indians' Man of the Year in 1949 and 1952, when he shared the award with Garcia and Wynn. He ranks third on the Indians all-time list in wins (207), innings pitched (2,850), strikeouts (1,277), starts (350), and shutouts (31). He ranks fourth in appearances (460) and complete games (188)

Bob Lemon (left) helps actor Ronald Reagan prepare for his role as Grover Cleveland Alexander in the film The Winning Team.

and fifth in winning percentage at .618 (207–128). He led the American League in wins three times, complete games five times, innings pitched four times, shutouts one time, and strikeouts one time. His only no-hitter came on June 30, 1948, at Detroit.

TRIVIA

Who holds the major league record for home runs by a pitcher?

Answers to the trivia questions are on pages 167–168.

In an ironic twist, given the fact that he became a pitcher because he wasn't a good batter, Lemon has the highest career batting average for a pinch-hitting pitcher with at least 100 at-bats. According to *The Great Book of Baseball Knowledge* by David Nemec, as a left-handed hitter, Lemon had 31 hits in 109 at bats—.284. He also had 37 home runs, one short of the record for a pitcher.

After his successful pitching career was over in 1958, Lemon moved into the managerial ranks. He managed Kansas City from 1970 to 1972, going 207–218 and winning the 1971 AL Manager of the Year award, then moved on to the Chicago White Sox in 1977–78, where he went 124–112 and was named the 1977 AL Manager of the Year. In 1978 he took over the New York Yankees after Billy Martin resigned and led them from a 14-game deficit to a World Series victory over the Los Angeles Dodgers. He managed parts of three more seasons with New York, going 34–31 with the Yankees in 1979, 11–14 in 1981, when they lost to the Dodgers in the World Series, and 6–8 in 1982. Although no longer managing, he remained on Yankees owner George Steinbrenner's payroll until his death on January 11, 2000, in Long Beach at the age of 79 after struggling with diabetes and several strokes.

"It was with tremendous sadness that I learned of the passing of Bob Lemon," Steinbrenner told the Associated Press. "He was an idol of mine when he pitched for the Indians, and he has been a true friend of many years. When our team was going through the turmoil in the 1978 season, he was just what we needed."

Lemon was inducted into the Baseball Hall of Fame in 1976 and had his No. 21 retired by the Indians in 1998.

Al Rosen:
Oh, So Close

It is impossible to come closer to a Triple Crown in baseball than Al Rosen did in 1953.

It came down to one step, a few inches at most, after a 3–2 count in his last at-bat of the season against Detroit's Al Aber. Rosen hit a chopper to third and lunged for the bag. He didn't make it, and he didn't complain.

"I was out," Rosen said in a telephone interview from his home in Southern California shortly after being inducted into the Indians Hall of Fame in the summer of 2006. "The umpire called it correctly."

When Rosen was thrown out on that play, he lost the batting title to Washington's Mickey Vernon, who went 2-for-4 on the last day of the season for a .337 average that just bettered Rosen's .336. Had he made it, Rosen would have won the batting title .3372 to .3371. Rosen, the Indians third baseman, still led the league with 43 home runs and 145 RBIs and was the unanimous choice for American League MVP that season.

Rosen, 82, said he didn't dwell on what might have been.

"It couldn't get any closer," said Rosen, who said no one was updating him on what Vernon was doing that day. "It was very disappointing. My teammates were disappointed. They all thought I was safe at first base. But I wasn't. My main emphasis was getting as many hits as I could. My focus was to do the best I could and I just came up short.

"As a kid growing up, I was inspired to be a major league player. But I never thought in my wildest dreams that I'd lead the league in home runs or set a home-run record for rookies (37 in 1950). There were a lot of milestones for me, and this was just the culmination of them. The idea that I could possibly win a Triple Crown was beyond imagination. I've had a lot of good times in my baseball career, and I focus on those as opposed to those that disappointed me. I'm pretty resilient. I don't look back. I always look forward. I was hoping for a better year the next year. Unfortunately, things happened beyond my control that shortened my baseball career. I do feel that I didn't complete the job that I wanted to complete."

Rosen, 5'10½" and 180 pounds, who had earned the nickname "Flip" as a softball pitcher while growing up in Miami, had replaced

Al Rosen just missed winning baseball's elusive Triple Crown in 1953 before injuries shortened his promising career.

Ken Keltner as the Indians third baseman but agreed to move to first base in 1954 to make room for rookie Rudy Regalado. In the middle of the season he broke his right index finger but continued to play, and by all accounts he had another great season, batting .300 with 24 home runs and 102 RBIs as the Indians won 111 games before being swept by the New York Giants in the 1954 World Series. During the All-Star Game in Cleveland, he hit two home runs and a single and had five RBIs as the American League won, 11–9. But he knew the broken finger caused him to alter his grip.

"It was never the same," he said. "I didn't have the right-hand pop I had before."

Then an auto accident before spring training in 1955 resulted in back and neck problems.

"Once you're playing hurt, you do other things," he said. "I had hamstring pulls and things of that nature. This debilitated me. I just finally decided after the 1956 season I wasn't the same player. I couldn't do something if I wasn't able to do it at my best. I didn't want to be one of those players who was traded from team to team and you wind up in a utility role or pinch hitting, so I just decided to pack it in.

"That I regret."

What the four-time All-Star regrets is that his career wasn't nearly as long as it could have been. He knows that wouldn't happen if he was playing today.

"If I were a player in today's world, they wouldn't have allowed me to play with a broken finger," said Rosen, who was respected for his toughness as a player. "The following year when I had this bad back and neck problem, I just went about my business getting ready for the season. In today's world that wouldn't be allowed. The club would protect their property much better. If a player gets hit on the foot by a foul tip, right away he goes to the hospital for an X-ray. In those days, it was really different. Everybody lived by the Wally Pipp rule: Don't get out of the lineup or Lou Gehrig will take your place.

"I don't blame the club at all. Primarily it was my own stubbornness. I wasn't going to allow injuries to stop me. I was wrong. I wouldn't have that choice playing in today's world."

After retiring as a player in 1956, Rosen went into the investment business in Cleveland, but he maintained his baseball ties. He went to spring training as a batting instructor with the Indians, and he served on the board of directors. He was part of George Steinbrenner's bid to buy the Indians in 1972. When that didn't happen, Steinbrenner bought the Yankees instead, and in 1978 he invited Rosen to become the club's president and general manager. The Yankees won the World Series in

TRIVIA

Who broke Al Rosen's Indians record of four grand slams in a season?

Answers to the trivia questions are on pages 167–168.

1978. Rosen served in a similar role in Houston from 1981 to 1985 and in San Francisco from 1986 to 1992. The Giants won the National League pennant in 1989.

Rosen was born on February 29, 1924, in Spartanburg, South Carolina. Though his family celebrated his birthday every March 1, he has seen February 29 only 20 times.

"I'll be 21 pretty soon," he said, laughing. "I'll be able to do a lot of things I couldn't do when I was 20."

1954: Surprising Sweep

The 1954 Indians were a powerful team. There was nothing they couldn't do.

Pitcher Bob Lemon went 23–7 to lead a staff that included Early Wynn (23–11), Mike Garcia (19–8), Art Houtteman (15–7), Bob Feller (13–3), and sterling relievers Ray Narleski and Don Mossi.

Second baseman Bobby Avila won the American League batting title with a .341 average. Center fielder Larry Doby led the AL with 32 home runs and 126 RBIs.

They won a then-record 111 games during the regular season and were in first place all but four days since May 16.

Of course, the New York Giants had center fielder Willie Mays, the National League batting champion at .345 with 41 home runs and 110 RBIs.

When it was all said and done, it was the Giants who became the second National League team to sweep to a most improbable World Series victory.

Game 1, Wednesday, September 29. At New York 5, Cleveland 2—Pinch-hitter Dusty Rhodes hit a three-run home run with one out in the tenth inning to lift the Giants and set the tone for the Series.

"I'd been holding Rhodes for just the spot, and when it came, I put him in," New York manager Leo Durocher told reporters after the game. "He really came through, too."

Said Rhodes to reporters, "I wasn't trying for a home run. I was just trying for a hit. It was the best hit I ever got in my life."

Vic Wertz went 4-for-5 for the Indians, and his first-inning triple with two outs scored Cleveland's first two runs. But the one at-bat in

IF ONLY . . . Gordon Cobbledick were a better prognosticator, Indians fans might have been a bit more prepared for the disappointing outcome of the four-game sweep by the New York Giants in the 1954 World Series. Cobbledick, then the sports editor of *The* (Cleveland) *Plain Dealer*, had predicted in a large headline on the front page of the sports section on September 28, "Indians Will Win in 6." His prediction was based in part on interviews he did with writers, broadcasters, and other baseball people before the ill-fated Series started.

which he went hitless became one of the most famous catches in major league baseball history. Mays turned in his famous over-the-left-shoulder basket catch in the eighth inning to snare Wertz's 460-foot drive.

"I slowed down when I started chasing it because I wanted to judge it right," Mays told reporters after the game. "You can't catch a ball going full speed. After I saw where it was going, and timed it, I went for it. As soon as I caught it—I took the ball over my left shoulder—I had to put out my hand to stop myself from crashing into that fence. Then I threw it back in.

"Say, that guy sure hits them a long way, doesn't he?"

Said Durocher to reporters after the game, "I can only say that it was one of the greatest catches I ever saw."

Game 2, Thursday, September 30. At New York 3, Cleveland 1—Rhodes hit another home run and a single and drove in two runs for the Giants, collecting half of the team's four hits. The Indians took a quick 1–0 lead when Al Smith led off the game with a home run, and the Indians did get eight hits off left-hander Johnny Antonelli. But they could not string enough of them together to do any real damage.

"They got their hits when it counted," Indians manager Al Lopez told reporters after the game. "We didn't."

Game 3, Friday, October 1. New York 6, at Cleveland 2—Mays had three hits and two RBIs, but it was Rhodes's pinch-hit single that scored two key runs in the third inning as the Giants built a 4–0 lead. Ruben Gomez and Hoyt Wilhelm combined to limit the Indians to four hits, one of them a home run by Wertz in the seventh inning. The Indians scored their only other run on a run-scoring ground ball by Smith, who reached on an error in the eighth inning.

"I ain't thinking about no records," Rhodes told reporters after tying a World Series record with three pinch-hits. "All I care about is seeing the Giants win it. I got enough to worry about, just trying to hit that ball—let alone bothering about records. But I sure would like to win this thing for Leo. He's a great guy."

Game 4, Saturday, October 2. New York 7, at Cleveland 4— The Giants built a 7–0 lead in the fifth inning thanks to two RBIs apiece by Monte Irvin and Wes Westrum off Lemon, who was pitching on two days' rest. The Indians scored three runs in the bottom of the fifth on a pinch-hit home run by Hank Majeski. Another pinch-hitter, Rudy Regalado, knocked in the Indians' other run with a single in the seventh. But it was the Giants who celebrated their fifth World Series title, their first since 1933.

Batting champions Bobby Avila of the Indians and Willie Mays of the National League champion New York Giants pose with their bats at the Polo Grounds in New York City on September 28, 1954, prior to the World Series opener.

By the NUMBERS

1954 World Series

.190—Indians' batting average in the World Series

2—Home runs hit by Dusty Rhodes in the World Series

3—Home runs hit by the Indians in the World Series

6.75—Bob Lemon's earned-run average in the World Series

9—Runs scored by the Indians in the World Series

21—Runs scored by the Giants in the World Series

"There was never any question in my mind that we'd win the world championship," Alvin Dark told reporters after the game. "It was something you can't put your finger on, but you just know.

"Don't be too hard on the Indians. They're a fine ballclub. It's just that we had a club that simply wouldn't be beaten. I doubt if there ever was a club that could have beaten us in this series.

"That's the kind of club we had all year—great pitching, fine defense, and timely hitting. We make a few runs, save a few, and then hold them off with good pitching."

Said Al Lopez of the Giants, "They played championship base-ball. They were good offensively and defensively, and their pitching was terrific. Their relief pitching especially was great.... We just weren't hitting, though. That may have had something to do with how good they looked."

A Winning Score

Generations of Indians fans grew up listening to Herb Score. For 34 years, whether on television or radio, Score filled in the fans on the fortunes of their favorite team. He was straightforward and professional, never too emotional, never too critical.

Parents remembered him from his playing days as a left-handed phenom, the 1955 American League Rookie of the Year often compared to Sandy Koufax. Children who never knew about his playing days tucked forbidden radios under their pillows, Score's soft New York accent describing the action from a late game on the West Coast putting them to sleep like a lullaby.

So what if he made a few mistakes during the broadcasts? He corrected himself and continued, always keeping the focus on the game he loved. He never inserted himself into the broadcast, never talked about his all-too-brief pitching career with the team, never referred to the tragic accident that befell him in 1957.

After so many years as the voice of the team, it was a cruel twist that when Score was inducted into the Indians Hall of Fame on a hot night in July 2006, he was unable to speak, unable to address the adoring crowd that greeted him with a standing ovation.

A number of medical problems followed Score's retirement from the broadcast booth after the Indians lost to the Florida Marlins in seven games in the 1997 World Series. A year later, Score was severely injured in an automobile accident in New Philadelphia, Ohio, about 80 miles south of Cleveland. On his way to Florida, where he and his wife, Nancy, spend their winters, Score pulled out in front of a tractor-trailer, which hit him broadside. Score suffered bruises to his brain and lungs, cuts on his face, a broken bone above

DID YOU KNOW . . . That Herb Score had two rules he lived by in broadcasting? According to former Indians announcer Nev Chandler in Terry Pluto's book *The Curse of Rocky Colavito*, Score's rules were (1) Never say *we*. The team was Cleveland, the Indians, or the Tribe—never *we* or *us*. (2) Don't be quick to second-guess or judge. Sometimes there is a good reason a guy made a bad play.

his eye, and three broken ribs. He recovered from that, but suffered a stroke. Then he fell and broke his shoulder and got a staph infection. Now his voice is barely a whisper, and he needs a walker or wheelchair.

The most touching part of the Indians Hall of Fame induction ceremony was that his roommate and best friend during their playing days with the Indians, Rocky Colavito, was also inducted and was right next to him, protectively hovering and tenderly maneuvering his wheelchair so Score could see the video highlights on the scoreboard behind him and then turn back to face the crowd.

Tom Hamilton, who worked with Score on the radio starting in 1990 and then succeeded him as the voice of the Indians, was the emcee of the ceremony, and he choked up talking about Score before the induction began.

"I've got very deep feelings for Herb," Hamilton said. "My first year in the big leagues, he treated me as an equal and there was no reason for him to do that. I'll never forget the way he treated me. What could have been a tough situation, he made enjoyable and comfortable from Day One. I'm eternally grateful for that.

"Think about it. For 30 years minimum, he was the most identifiable Cleveland Indian. For a 30-year stretch, ownership changed constantly, players changed constantly. Whenever you had a good player, he didn't stay here. But the one constant was always Herb. For a good 30 years, if you said, 'Cleveland Indians,' I think the first person people thought of was Herb. He was always there through thick and thin."

Mike Hargrove, former player and manager of the Indians who is now manager of the Seattle Mariners, watched the ceremony from across the diamond. He fully understood what Score meant to the Indians, and vice versa.

IF ONLY . . . Cleveland Indians fans live by the phrases "what if?" and "if only." But in the case of Score, either phrase is totally appropriate, although he personally would never allow himself to think that way.

If only he hadn't been hit in the eye, what might the future have held for Score and the Indians? What if he hadn't hurt his arm trying to come back the next season?

He was a 20-game winner at the age of 23. Though the Indians stumbled to sixth and fourth places in 1957 and 1958, respectively, they finished second in 1959, when Score went 9–11. Had he not been injured, he'd have been in his prime. Another 20 victories would not have been out of the question, and the 11-game difference might have allowed the Indians to overtake Chicago that season. On the other hand, "Trader" Frank Lane had come to Cleveland in 1958, and no player was safe. So even if Score had regained his form, he might not have stayed in Cleveland long enough for the Indians to reap the benefits.

"With any franchise, there are faces from the past and present that represent who they are as a team," Hargrove said before the ceremony. "I think Herbie is one of those guys, along with Bob Feller, Larry Doby, and people like that."

When Score burst onto the major league scene in 1955, there was every reason to believe he'd be mentioned in the same breath as the other Indians greats. He had already survived some difficulties. Born in Rosedale, New York, on June 7, 1933, he was hit by a truck when he was three years old. His legs were crushed, and doctors told his parents he'd never walk again. But he recovered completely and also survived rheumatic fever a few years later. His parents separated when Score was a freshman in high school, and he and his two sisters moved to Lake Worth, Florida, with their mother.

Score was just out of high school when he was signed by Indians scout Cy Slapnicka, who had discovered Bob Feller a few years earlier. By 1954, Score, playing for Indianapolis, was the MVP in the American Association with a 22–5 record and 2.62 ERA with 330 strikeouts in 251 innings. The Indians brought him up in 1955, and he went 16–10 with a 2.85 ERA, striking out 245 batters to lead the AL and set a rookie record that stood until 1984, when it was broken by Dwight Gooden. In 1956 Score went 20–9 with a 2.53 ERA and a league-leading 263 strikeouts.

He and Colavito, who started rooming together in Indianapolis, became almost inseparable. Devout Catholics, they eschewed the nightlife on the road, although Score never could get Colavito to share his passion for reading.

Here were two up-and-coming stars who were worthy role models for the youngsters who adored them.

But everything changed on May 7, 1957, when Score, just 23, was hit in the right eye by a line drive off the bat of Gil McDougald of the New York Yankees in the first inning of a game at Cleveland Municipal Stadium. Score went down as if shot, and blood spurted from his eye, nose, and mouth.

Herb Score delivers a pitch while striking out 16 Boston Red Sox batters as the Indians win the second game of a doubleheader in Cleveland on May 1, 1955.

"As soon as I hit the ground, I prayed to St. Jude," said Score, whose middle name is Jude. "I was afraid I wouldn't be able to see."

He told Hal Lebovitz of the *Cleveland News,* "I've been in pain before, but this is the worst. I feel like screaming."

McDougald was equally upset. Fearing Score would lose his eye, he got frequent updates from the hospital on Score's condition.

Score, 2–1 with a 2.00 ERA at the time of the injury, was in the hospital for three weeks and lost the rest of the season, but he returned in 1958. Unfortunately, his fastball was never the same, though he always blamed a torn elbow tendon suffered that spring and not the eye injury. He went 2–3 with a 3.95 ERA and 48 strikeouts in 1958 and was 9–11 with a 4.71 ERA and 147 strikeouts in 1959. He was traded to Chicago for pitcher Barry Latman on April 18, 1960, a day after Colavito was traded to Detroit. Score actually thought he was going to Detroit with Colavito until a bad outing in spring training probably caused the Tigers to change their minds. Score went 6–12 with the White Sox from 1960 to 1962 before retiring. When the Indians asked him to fill in on some television broadcasts in 1963, he took them up on their offer and stayed for the next 34 years.

Cleveland Rocks

It has been almost 50 years, and Rocky Colavito is still upset about the Easter Sunday trade that sent him from Cleveland to Detroit on April 17, 1960.

"If you think I still hold a grudge, you're right," Colavito said during a roundtable discussion the day before he was inducted into the Indians Hall of Fame on July 29, 2006. I didn't want to give [General Manager Frank Lane] the satisfaction of thinking that I couldn't handle it. But I was in a terrible funk."

So were the devastated Indians fans who had taken the New Yorker to their hearts like one of their own. He was a handsome, wholesome slugger who was coming into his prime at 26. He'd hit 41 home runs in 1958 and 42 in 1959. Little kids all over Cleveland imitated his batting routine, starting by lifting the bat over their heads and putting it behind their shoulders and stretching.

Then all of a sudden, he was gone, sent to Detroit for Harvey Kuenn, 29, who had led the American League in hitting with a .353 batting average in 1959.

In the season opener against Cleveland two days later, Colavito went 0-for-6, striking out four times, although the Tigers beat the Indians, 4–2.

"I had one of those fantastic days," Colavito said. "I struck out four times, I hit into a double play, and I popped out. That was the worst day in my professional career. In fact, even my life.

"I really believe this. I think if I would have stayed here, I think my numbers would have been much better. If I would have never been moved around, with the shock of the trades, I think all my numbers would have been better. I don't know that to be a fact, don't get me wrong. But if I would have stayed here, I would have been at home, I would have played longer. I retired at 35. I've never been drunk in my life. I don't mean that as a brag. But the bottom line is that I took care of myself. I wasn't nearly ready to retire. But when you start getting bounced around and you know you can play, it's tough."

Rocky Colavito says he's still bothered by the Easter Sunday trade that sent him out of Cleveland in 1960.

Tough described Colavito and his life before he became a major leaguer, too.

Colavito was born on August 10, 1933, in the Bronx. As the son of Italian immigrants growing up close to Yankee Stadium, it was no surprise he adored Joe DiMaggio, imitating his batting stance and asking to wear DiMaggio's No. 5.

Colavito was the youngest of five children. His mother died when he was nine years old. Money was tight, so the young Colavito contributed by taking a job as a delivery boy for a pharmacy and a fruit store. He also earned money playing pool.

But baseball was always his love. He played whenever he could and always planned to be a professional player when he grew up, although he did try to take some classes in auto mechanics—just in case. But the classes at Samuel Gompers Trade

TRIVIA

Who beat out Rocky Colavito in the 1956 Rookie of the Year voting?

Answers to the trivia questions are on pages 167–168.

School were full, and he transferred to Roosevelt High School. When he was 16, he was spotted by a Cleveland scout. Because of his age and his family's situation, he was granted a special waiver so the Indians could sign him before his high school class graduated. Despite interest from the Philadelphia Phillies and Athletics and the hometown Yankees—all of whom looked at him as a pitching prospect—Colavito signed with the Indians early in 1951, and he went to his first spring training three months later. The Indians thought of him as a pitcher, too, because of his arm strength and because his flat feet made him a slow runner.

He pitched four innings in one game for Daytona Beach, giving up one run and one hit, striking out three and walking three, for an earned-run average of 2.52. But he also led the Florida State League with 23 home runs and tied for the league lead with 140 games in center field. He batted .275 with a league-leading 303 putouts and also tied for the league lead with 20 errors.

In 1952 he split time between Cedar Rapids and Spartanburg, and in 1953, he was promoted to Reading, where Manager Kerby Farrell suggested he abandon his DiMaggio impression, close his stance, and crouch down a bit at the plate. As a result, he led the league with 28 home runs and 121 RBIs. More importantly, he met the woman who would become his wife—Carmen Perrotti.

In 1954 Colavito played at Indianapolis, where he roomed with hot pitching prospect Herb Score. Colavito batted .271 and led the league with 38 home runs. After the season he married Carmen, and the next spring he joined the major leaguers at training camp but was reassigned to Indianapolis. He batted .268 with 30 home runs and 104 RBIs and was called up to Cleveland at the end of the 1955 season. He had four hits in nine at-bats, a respectable .444 average. In 1956 he broke camp with the Indians, although they were still working on getting him to change his batting stance, even employing the legendary Tris Speaker to assist in the effort. In June Colavito was sent down to San Diego, where he batted .368 in 35 games. After he was recalled, he had three hits and three RBIs in his first game back, en route to season totals of 21 home runs, 65 RBIs, and a .276 batting average. In 1957 his numbers improved to 25 home runs and 84 RBIs, but his batting average dipped to .252.

When Joe Gordon replaced Bobby Bragan as manager in the middle of the 1958 season, he continued to tinker with Colavito's approach to batting. Gordon told him to wait on the ball and hit straight away instead of pulling the ball. He encouraged him to hit singles instead of swinging for the fences every time up. With that in mind, Colavito batted a career high .303, with 41 home runs and 113 RBIs and was voted the Indians' Man of the Year by the writers. He also played some first base and even pitched in a game, but 1958 will be remembered as the year Colavito really became a power hitter. The only possible downside, according to Gordon Cobbledick's book *Don't Knock the Rock*, was that after hitting a home run, Colavito shook the hand of practically every teammate or coach he could find, squeezing so hard they feared the gesture.

Of course, the key development in Colavito's career came off the field that season when "Trader" Frank Lane was hired as the Indians general manager before the 1958 season. He'd been run out of St. Louis after trading popular local product Red Schoendienst and trying to trade the incomparable Stan Musial. In Cleveland, legend has it that Bragan put a curse on the Indians when he was fired. But

By the NUMBERS

12—Number of times Indians have led the AL in slugging percentage.

Name	Year	Slugging Percentage
Nap Lajoie	1903	.518
Nap Lajoie	1904	.552
Elmer Flick	1905	.462
Joe Jackson	1913	.551
Tris Speaker	1916	.502
Larry Doby	1952	.541
Al Rosen	1953	.613
Rocky Colavito	1958	.620
Albert Belle	1995	.690
Manny Ramirez	1999	.663
Manny Ramirez	2000	.697
Jim Thome	2002	.677

others blame Lane for the downfall of a franchise that didn't rebound until the mid-1990s.

After his performance in 1958, Colavito held out before signing for the 1959 season, a move that didn't sit well with Lane. Of course, Colavito proved his worth once again with 111 RBIs, and he tied Washington's Harmon Killebrew for the league lead with 42 home runs, including a record-tying four in a game on June 10 in Baltimore, a tough place to hit one home run, let alone four. He'd gone into the game in a slump amid newspaper reports he was about to be traded. He finished the season in Cleveland with a .257 batting average, however, and Lane focused on that during negotiations for Colavito's 1960 contract. After another holdout, Colavito finally signed as spring training was about to begin.

But he was gone before the season started. One day later, so was Score, sent to the White Sox for Barry Latman. Some have suggested the insecure Lane was jealous of their popularity. But that seems too easy an answer for all of Lane's manipulations. After all, this was a

DID YOU KNOW ...

That when Frank Lane traded Colavito and Herb Score on back-to-back days in 1960, the entire Indians roster had turned over since Lane's arrival in 1958?

man who fired Joe Gordon when the Indians faltered in the 1959 pennant race and tried to hire Leo Durocher. But when Lane couldn't make a deal with Durocher, he rehired Gordon two days after he fired him—giving him a two-year contract and a raise. Later on he traded Gordon to Detroit for Manager Jimmy Dykes.

While Kuenn played one season in Cleveland before Lane sent him to San Francisco, Colavito spent four productive seasons in Detroit, never hitting fewer than 22 home runs, before he was traded to Kansas City, along with pitcher Bob Anderson and $50,000, for pitchers Ed Rakow and Dave Wickersham and second baseman Jerry Lumpe on November 18, 1963. Colavito had 34 home runs and 102 RBIs while batting .274 for the Athletics in 1964 before returning to Cleveland in a three-way deal involving the Athletics, White Sox, and Indians on January 20, 1965. Chicago sent outfielders Jim Landis and Mike Hershberger and pitcher Fred Talbot to Kansas City for Colavito. Then the Indians sent pitcher Tommy John, catcher John Romano, and outfielder Tommie Agee to the White Sox for Colavito, who would lead the league in 1965 with 108 RBIs and was again voted the Indians' Man of the Year.

It was a move borne of desperation. The Indians had drawn 1.5 million fans before the trade of Colavito and 950,000 the season after the deal. In 1963 attendance dropped to 562,507, and there was talk of the franchise moving to Seattle, Oakland, or Dallas. General Manager Gabe Paul figured he needed to do something, so he gave up a lot to get back the 32-year-old Colavito. Attendance did go up almost 300,000 as Colavito batted .287 with 26 home runs and led the league with 108 RBIs. In 1966 he hit 30 homers but was batting .238 with 72 RBIs. In 1967 he platooned with Leon Wagner in right field, clashed with Manager Joe Adcock, and finally was traded to the White Sox for Jimmy King and $50,000 on July 29, 1967. He batted .231 that season and .211 the next in 40 games with the Los Angeles Dodgers and 39 with the New York Yankees before retiring.

He Played in Cleveland?

In their 100-plus years of existence, the Cleveland Indians had dozens of players, such as Bob Feller and Mel Harder, who played their entire careers with the franchise. There were other players so closely tied to the team, like Rick Manning or Duane Kuiper or even Jim Thome and Omar Vizquel, that no matter where else their careers took them, they were best remembered for their time spent with the Indians.

But in more than 100 years, thousands of players have passed through Cleveland—and not of all them were the result of the nonstop deal-making by "Trader" Frank Lane, either.

Some of them were young prospects sent away too soon. Some of them were veterans just trying to hold on one more season. Most became much more famous playing elsewhere—either before or after they landed in Cleveland.

At any rate, only the truest, bluest fans will know that all of the following players spent some time with Cleveland. Chances are there's at least one name here that will cause readers to say, "I didn't know that."

Cy Young—The only pitcher to win more than 500 games, Denton True Young was born in Gilmore, Ohio, on March 29, 1867. He had been playing the infield for a team in Tuscarawas County, south of Akron, but he was pitching in Canton when Spiders secretary/treasurer Davis Hawley spotted him. Hawley bought Young's contract from Canton for $250. Nicknamed "Cy" because his fastball looked like a cyclone, Young earned $75 a month with the Spiders upon joining them in August 1890. In nine seasons with the Spiders, Young went 241–135, including a victory in the first game at League Park in 1891, and he helped the team win its only championship in 1895. Of course, he became more famous as the Boston Red Sox Hall of Famer who won the Triple Crown in 1901, when he led the American League with a 33–10 record, 1.62 earned-run average, and 158 strikeouts. He helped the Red Sox with the baseball championship in 1903 and pitched a perfect game against the Philadelphia Athletics in 1904. He returned to Cleveland to pitch from 1909 to 1911. Nowadays, the best pitcher in each league each season is presented the Cy Young Award. Young died in Newcomerstown, Ohio, on November 4, 1955.

"Shoeless" Joe Jackson—Jackson was acquired from Philadelphia in 1910. A native of South Carolina, he didn't like playing in the North, especially in a big East Coast city like Philadelphia. The Athletics had sent him to the minor leagues in Savannah and New Orleans with the hopes they could convince him to return to Philadelphia, but when they were unable to do so, they sent him to Cleveland for outfielder Bris Lord in 1910. He played only 20 games in Cleveland that season, but he batted .387. For the rest of his five years in Cleveland, all he did was hit. In 1911 he batted .408 with seven home runs and 83 RBIs. The .408 remains the highest single-season batting average in team history. In 1912 he batted .395 (second highest single-season batting average in team history) with 90 RBIs. In 1913 he batted .373; in 1914 it was .338. He was batting .327 when he was traded to the Chicago White Sox for three players (Braggo Roth, Larry Chappell, and Ed Klepfer) and $31,500 on August 21, 1915. Four years later, he was caught up in the Black Sox scandal, which involved Chicago players allegedly trying to fix the 1919 World Series. Although a jury acquitted Jackson and seven of his teammates in 1921, they were banned from baseball for life. Still, Jackson's .356 career batting average ranks him third in the history of the game. His .375 in his years with Cleveland is still the team record for career batting average, and he also holds the club records for hits in one season (233 in 1911) and triples in one season (26 in 1912). "Shoeless" Joe Jackson got his nickname because after wearing new shoes for one game early in his career, he developed painful blisters on his feet and played the next day in his socks, drawing jeers from the crowd. It was the only time he played without his shoes, but somehow the nickname stuck.

Satchel Paige—No one is quite sure how old Leroy Robert "Satchel" Paige was when he pitched for the Indians in 1948. Although he listed his birth date as July 7, 1906, he was never quite sure that was right. He was one of 11 children, and record-keeping in Mobile, Alabama, apparently left a little to be desired back in those days. As a boy, he had a job carrying luggage for train passengers, which is the source of his nickname. At any rate, he had been pitching for more than 20 years in the Negro Leagues when Cleveland owner Bill Veeck signed Paige on his 42nd birthday—July 7, 1948—about a year after Veeck had made Larry Doby the first African American player in the American League. Many criticized Veeck for the move, thinking he'd done it for the publicity. But Paige put most of that talk to rest by going 6–1 with a 2.48 earned-run average in

Satchel Paige, signed by Indians president Bill Veeck from the Kansas City Monarchs of the Negro American League, helped the Tribe to the American League pennant in 1948.

14—Number of general managers the Indians have had through the years.

1903–27 Ernest S. Barnard

1916–17 Bob McRoy

1927–35 Billy Evans

1935–41 C.C. Slapnicka

1941–46 Roger Peckinpaugh

1946–49 Bill Veeck

1950–57 Hank Greenberg

1957–61 Frank Lane

1961–73 Gabe Paul

1973–85 Phil Seghi

1985–87 Joe Klein

1987–91 Hank Peters

1991–2001 John Hart

2001–present Mark Shapiro

1948, helping the team win the World Series. He was 4–7 with an earned-run average of 3.04 in 1949. Of course, Veeck couldn't help but love the fact that Paige was the consummate entertainer on the mound and with the media in the clubhouse. His first start, a 5–3 victory over Washington on August 3, 1948, drew 72,434 fans, and when he beat Chicago 1–0 on August 20, the team drew a major league single-game record 78,382. Paige was elected to the Hall of Fame in 1971, the first player so honored based primarily on his statistics in the Negro Leagues.

Billy Martin—Alfred Manuel "Billy" Martin already had quite the reputation by the time he played for the Indians in 1959. The infielder had been traded by the New York Yankees to Kansas City after being involved in a nightclub brawl, and after one season, Kansas City traded him to Detroit. But Frank Lane was looking for a feisty leader, and he thought Martin would be just the guy. So on November 20, 1958, Lane sent pitchers Don Mossi and Ray Narleski and shortstop Ossie Alvarez to Detroit for Martin and pitcher Al

Cicotte. Martin played in 73 games at second or third base and hit .260 with nine home runs and 24 RBIs. He had 63 hits and scored 37 runs. That apparently wasn't enough. After the season, Lane sent Martin, pitcher Cal McLish, and first baseman Gordy Coleman to Cincinnati for second baseman Johnny Temple. Martin also played for Milwaukee and Minnesota before retiring in 1961. He became best known for his off-field battles and his love/hate relationship with owner George Steinbrenner while managing the Yankees five different times and winning the World Series in 1977. Martin was 61 when he died in a car crash on Christmas Day, 1989.

Roger Maris—The native of Hibbing, Minnesota, who grew up in North Dakota passed up a football scholarship to the University of Oklahoma and signed with the Indians for a $5,000 bonus in 1953. After a few seasons in the minor leagues, he batted .235 with 14 home runs and 51 RBIs with the Indians in 1957. He tailed off to .225 with nine home runs and 27 RBIs in 51 games in 1958 and was a backup for Rocky Colavito in right field. After a couple of run-ins with Lane, he was traded, along with pitcher Dick Tomanek and first baseman Preston Ward, to the Kansas City Athletics for first baseman Vic Power and shortstop Woodie Held on June 15, 1958. He became an All-Star with Kansas City in 1959, but in spite of that, Kansas City traded him to the New York Yankees after the season. He became the American League MVP in 1960 and 1961 and was named the major league Player of the Year in 1961, when he hit a then major league single-season record 61 home runs (since broken by Mark McGwire with 70 in 1998 and Barry Bonds with 73 in 2001.) Maris died of lymphatic cancer in 1985.

Boog Powell—John Wesley "Boog" Powell's best days were behind him when he was obtained, along with pitcher Don Hood, from Baltimore on February 25, 1975, for catcher Dave Duncan and outfielder Alvin McGrew. Powell, a first baseman, had been a four-time All-Star, the 1970 American League MVP, and a two-time World Series champion with Baltimore,

TRIVIA

If "Shoeless" Joe Jackson's career batting average of .356 ranks third in baseball history, whose career batting averages rank first and second?

Answers to the trivia questions are on pages 167–168.

where he played with Indians player/manager Frank Robinson. With the Indians, Powell hit .297 with 27 home runs in 1975. When his average dropped to .215 in 1976, he was released.

Graig Nettles—This was pretty much the classic Indians trade. Nettles was an up-and-coming star when he was acquired, along with outfielder Ted Uhlaender and pitchers Dean Chance and Bob Miller, from Minnesota for pitchers Luis Tiant and Stan Williams on December 11, 1969. The Indians gave up on Tiant too soon, then didn't recognize what they had in Nettles and sent him away, too, only to watch him bloom in, of course, New York. Minnesota actually used Nettles in the outfield, but he was to become a great defensive third baseman. He batted just .235, .261, and .253 in his three seasons in Cleveland, although he was named the Indians' Man of the Year in 1971. The Indians had groomed their own third baseman in a young Buddy Bell, so Nettles became expendable. He and catcher Jerry Moses were sent to the Yankees for catcher John Ellis, outfielders Charles Spikes and Rusty Torres, and second baseman Jerry Kenney on November 27, 1972. He became a six-time All-Star, two-time Golden Glove winner, and two-time World Series champion. He holds the American League record for home runs by a third baseman with 319.

Chris Chambliss—You'd have thought the Indians might have learned something from the Graig Nettles trade, but they made a similar move with first baseman Chambliss one year later. The difference between the players was that Chambliss, a native of Dayton, Ohio, had come up through the Indians farm system. He was a first-round pick by the Indians in 1970 and won the American Association's Rookie of the Year award that season when he batted .342 for Wichita. He batted .275 with the Indians and was named the American League Rookie of the Year in 1971. He hit .292 in 1972, .273 in 1973, and was batting .328 when the Indians sent him and pitchers Dick Tidrow and Cecil Upshaw to the Yankees for pitchers Fritz Peterson, Fred Beene, Tom Buskey, and Steve Kline in a trade on April 27, 1974. Like Nettles, Chambliss became a star for the Yankees and a two-time World Series champion.

Fritz Peterson/Mike Kekich—From a purely baseball standpoint, there would be no reason to remember either Fritz Peterson

23 games in 1987. But the Indians won just 61 games that season, so Carlton had ½ of their wins before being traded July 31 to the Minnesota Twins for a player to be named later, which turned out to be minor leaguer Jeff Perry. Most of Carlton's accomplishments came before he arrived. The left-hander starred with St. Louis from 1965 to 1971, winning a World Series championship in 1967. He was traded to Philadelphia before the 1972 season and enjoyed the best years of his career there, despite an ongoing feud with the media. Carlton was the first pitcher to win the Cy Young Award four times, in 1972, 1977, 1980, and 1982, plus another World Series title in 1980. He won 329 games, second only to Warren Spahn among left-handers. He struck out 4,136, fourth all time. He shares the National League strikeout record for a single game—19.

Was Gaylord Perry All Wet?

Pitcher Gaylord Perry didn't leave much to the imagination when he titled his 1974 autobiography *Me and the Spitter: An Autobiographical Confession.*

After years of questions and accusations, Perry came clean. Well, not literally.

But in an amusing tale written with Cleveland sportswriter Bob Sudyk, Perry revealed the who, what, where, when, and why of his career with the spitball.

The book opens with a copy of the baseball rules for pitchers as they read in 1974. What follows is a detailed description of how Perry broke them.

According to the book, Perry threw his first spitball in competition against the New York Mets in a marathon doubleheader on May 31, 1964, at Shea Stadium. He was pitching in relief for the San Francisco Giants in the second game in front of a crowd of 57,037, most of whom had no idea what he was doing.

Even without the debut of Perry's spitter, the doubleheader was historic—and not just because Willie Mays took a turn at shortstop or because the Mets pulled off a triple play. After the Giants won the first game 5–3 in nine innings, they took a 6–1 lead in the nightcap, only to watch the Mets come back and tie the score at 6–6 in the seventh inning. Sixteen innings would follow. The combined 32 innings set a record for two games in one day, as did the nine hours and 52 minutes it took to complete them. The nightcap took seven hours and 23 minutes to complete, also a record for one game. Fans who arrived at the stadium for the 1:00 PM start were heading home around midnight. The players and umpires were dead on their feet.

This was the situation Perry found himself in when he entered the game in the bottom of the thirteenth inning. He was the only pitcher the Giants had left, save for Bob Hendley, who was scheduled to start the next day. Perry, 25, brought a 2–1 record and a 4.77 earned-run average with him, but he clearly felt his livelihood was at stake. After spending the better part of six years in the minor leagues, he was 1–6 in 31 games with the Giants in 1963. He had a fastball and a curve, but neither was so overpowering that his future in baseball was assured.

Admitted spitballer Gaylord Perry won 70 games over four seasons with the Indians.

That when Gaylord and Jim faced each other on July 3, 1973, it was the first time in American League history brothers had squared off? Jim's Tigers beat Gaylord's Indians, 5–4.

So, when Jim Hickman singled to lead off the fifteenth inning and moved to second on a sacrifice, catcher Tommy Haller called time and approached the mound. "Gaylord, it's time to try it out," Perry wrote in his autobiography. Haller was talking about the game, but he might as well have been talking about the stage of Perry's career as well.

With Chris Cannizzaro at bat, Perry threw one spitter that dropped too low and followed that with another that did the same thing. Cannizzaro fouled the next pitch off umpire Ed Sudol's foot. When the ball came back to Perry on the mound, it was still wet, so he threw it again and Cannizzaro swung and missed.

Mets manager Casey Stengel started yelling from the dugout, accusing Perry of throwing spitballs. Meanwhile, Perry looked at his infielders who had "that look of pride you get from your folks on graduation day." Perry eventually walked Cannizzaro, but while Giants manager Alvin Dark was complaining about a checked swing, the disgruntled fans went nuts, and in all the commotion, Perry took the opportunity to spit right on the baseball.

Mets pitcher Galen Cisco was the next batter. He hit a ball back to Perry that was still so wet that it slipped out of Perry's hand as he threw to second base. Still, the Giants got a double play out of it and ended the inning.

Things were going along, well, swimmingly, though Perry was beginning to flag. Before he went out for the twentieth inning, someone gave him a slippery elm tablet, which increased his saliva production. Eventually, the Giants won 8–6 in the twenty-third inning and a legend was born.

"During the next eight years, I reckon I tried everything on the old apple but salt and pepper and chocolate sauce toppin'," Perry wrote.

Perry said he learned how to throw a spitball from veteran Bob Shaw, but he said Shaw would deny that. According to Perry, deception was all part of the act. He'd make a big show of licking his first two fingers and then juggling the rosin bag or wiping the fingers dry on his uniform. However, he became an expert at avoiding those fingers with the rosin bag or spitting on his thumb and then rewetting the fingers after he appeared to have dried them off. A fidgeter on the mound, Perry also would fake going to his mouth just to keep batters guessing.

The extra moisture on a spitball made it break much more severely than a normal pitch. Basically, though, there wasn't much to it. Perry said all he needed was "three slippery elm tablets to suck on, two damp fingers, the skill of an actor, and the guts of a burglar."

Over the years, people tried everything to catch Perry. He was asked to take off his pants, cap, shirt, and shoes. Umpires checked his gloves, belts, and towels. He was filmed and photographed in slow motion. When Billy Martin was the manager in Detroit, he had a bloodhound sniff around for Vaseline.

In addition to plain old spit, Perry experimented with Vaseline, KY jelly, baby oil, suntan lotion, and hair tonics, placing them on his cap, pants, shirt, belt, neck, forehead, wrist, ear, hair—the little he had—and the tongue of his shoe. He always had the stuff in two places, in case the umpires found one.

"I never wanted to be out there without anything," he wrote in his autobiography. "It wouldn't be professional."

After all the experimentation, Perry settled on Vaseline. Ironically, he said he perfected his first "grease ball" in a spring training game against Cleveland in 1968. Four years later, he and shortstop Frank Duffy would be traded to the Indians for pitcher Sam McDowell.

It turned out to be a great move for the Indians. Perry went 24–16, and eight of those losses were by one run. He pitched 342⅔ innings. He had 234 strikeouts, 82 walks, and a 1.92 earned-run average, becoming the only Indian to win the Cy Young Award. He was named the Indians' Man of the Year that year, an award he won again with his brother Jim in 1974.

TRIVIA

What were Jim's and Gaylord's nicknames in high school?

Answers to the trivia questions are on pages 167–168.

In four seasons with the Indians, Perry won 70 games before being traded to Texas on June 13, 1975, for pitchers Rick Waits, Jackie Brown, and Jim Bibby and $100,000. After leaving Cleveland, Perry pitched for Texas, the New York Yankees, Atlanta, Seattle, San Diego, and Kansas City. He became the only man to win the Cy Young Award in both leagues when his 21–6 record in 1978 earned him that honor in the National League. He won his 300th game with Seattle in 1982. Gaylord and Jim, who pitched with the Indians from 1959 to 1963 and 1974 to 1975, won a total of 529 games, second only to Phil and Joe Niekro's 539 victories in major league history.

Perry was elected to the Hall of Fame in 1991. It was quite an honor for a young man who'd grown up on a tobacco farm in North Carolina that had no indoor plumbing. He became a three-sport star at Williamston High School, forced into pitching instead of playing third base during the playoffs his freshman year. He was an all-state defensive end on the football team his sophomore and junior years before giving it up for fear of injury. He also averaged 30 points and 20 rebounds for the basketball team, earning a scholarship to Campbell College before the Giants asked him not to play to guard against injury.

Cleveland Makes History Again

Frank Robinson first joined the Indians as a player.

On September 12, 1974, General Manager Phil Seghi, who had been the assistant general manager in Cincinnati when Robinson came up through the Reds farm team and became the 1956 National League Rookie of the Year, traded for Robinson to help the Indians make a final push for the playoffs. It didn't work. Robinson batted just .200 in 15 games with two home runs and five RBIs, and the Indians finished 77–85, costing Ken Aspromonte his job.

The funny thing was, at least one New York reporter had written that Robinson would become the Indians manager in 1972, when they hired Aspromonte instead. But with the team struggling under Aspromonte, speculation about Robinson replacing him started as soon as Robinson joined the team.

It did not take long for the speculation to become reality. On October 3, 1974, Robinson became the first African American manager in Major League Baseball. It was a historic occasion, no less important than Jackie Robinson becoming the first black player in baseball in 1947 or Larry Doby becoming the first black player in the American League when he signed with the Indians three months later.

"I think it would have been one of Jackie's biggest thrills," Jackie Robinson's widow, Rachel, said when Frank Robinson (no relation) was hired. "He would have been ecstatic. Things didn't have to involve him personally for him to be excited."

Baseball commissioner Bowie Kuhn and American League president Lee MacPhail flew to Cleveland for Frank Robinson's press conference in the Stadium Club, where more than 100 reporters from all over the country packed in to record the event.

Kuhn called such a move "long overdue" while MacPhail said, "The impact of Frank Robinson being named manager of the Indians, the first black manager in major league history, is second in importance only to Jackie Robinson's entry into baseball in 1947."

Frank Robinson also paid tribute to baseball's pioneer.

"I don't know if I could go through what Jackie went through, and I thank the Lord for making him the kind of man he was," said Robinson, who would also serve as the team's designated hitter. "If I had only one wish that could be answered, it would be that Jackie Robinson could be here today."

As for his own place in history, Robinson tried to downplay it.

"I'm the first one only because I was born black."

Asked about the potentially sticky problem of firing a black manager, which some had used as an excuse not to hire one, Robinson said, "I don't see any problem in firing me or any black manager. If I'm not doing the job, I should be fired. And if I don't do the job and I'm fired, I don't think there'll be any real repercussions."

Seghi tried to take the notion of color out of the equation.

"Frank Robinson is here because he has all the qualities we've been searching for," Seghi told reporters. "I felt I wanted Frank because I wanted the very best man available. I had no reservations whatsoever about hiring him."

Public response to Robinson's hiring was generally positive, although there likely were less public pockets of negativity. The only real complication was that by hiring Robinson, the Indians bypassed Doby, a beloved figure in Cleveland who had been considered a front-runner for the job.

"I'm not resentful of anything, but I'm disappointed they didn't see fit to hire me," Doby said. "But I am happy that baseball is now showing it's not prejudiced.... I'm sure Jackie Robinson will be smiling when Robby is hired, because he's the reason it's all happening now."

Wrote Cleveland *Plain Dealer* sports editor Hal Lebovitz in a column the morning of the announcement, "Frank Robinson is a man whose time has come and who is entitled to the opportunity to which he has dedicated himself.... Because he is the first, there will

Frank Robinson speaks at a news conference in Cleveland after being named the major league's first black manager, in October 1974. Baseball commissioner Bowie Kuhn sits in the background.

be much made of the color of his skin in all the dispatches and tapes and films. As we wrote Sunday, he will be the first black manager at the start of the season—perhaps the first half—but after that, he'll no longer be unique. He'll simply become Frank Robinson, Manager. And he'll rise or fall, not on the color of his skin but on his ability, or lack of it, to handle pitchers; on his ability, or lack of it, to run a ball-club...personally I'm glad to see he is getting the opportunity.

"I would rather have a fresh, eager, deserving Robinson than some washed-out manager who has made the rounds. It's another exciting adventure in Cleveland baseball history, and I'm glad to be aboard for the ride. I hope all the fans look at it this way.... He is a man whose time has come and who has been given the opportunity. I wish him the very best. I hope every Indians fan does."

Well-wishers from throughout baseball praised the move.

By the
NUMBERS

Frank Robinson's Year-by-Year Managing Record

1975 Cleveland 79–80

1976 Cleveland 81–78

1977 Cleveland 26–31

1981 San Francisco 56–55

1982 San Francisco 87–75

1983 San Francisco 79–83

1984 San Francisco 42–64

1988 Baltimore 54–101

1989 Baltimore 87–75

1990 Baltimore 76–85

1991 Baltimore 13–24

2002 Montreal 83–79

2003 Montreal 83–79

2004 Montreal 67–95

2005 Washington 81–81

2006 Washington 71–91

Bill Veeck, the owner who signed Doby, said he was disappointed Doby didn't get the job, but he added, "I'm delighted somebody is finally becoming intelligent enough to select a manager on ability rather than his color. I'm glad to find a club where an unknown doesn't frighten them to death. That is the only reason for the hesitancy in hiring a black manager."

Added Earl Weaver, who managed Frank Robinson in Baltimore, "Frank is definitely ready to be a major league manager. I hope people judge him on his merits, not whether he is white or black. There is no doubt in my mind that he will do a good job."

Indians players were generally supportive, too.

"I think it's a hell of a move for black people," said Tom McCraw. "This compares to Jackie Robinson and Larry Doby getting their chances to play in the big leagues. But it's also a good move for the

Cleveland club. Nobody around here cares what color he is, and I have no doubt Frank will do a good job."

Said Dick Bosman, "If he manages the way he played—he'll do anything to beat you—I'm sure I'm going to like him very much."

Added Tom Buskey, "It doesn't make any difference if he's black or white. Not to me it doesn't. I don't particularly like the idea of him trying to be a designated hitter and manager, because I think managing requires 100 percent concentration. But maybe he is capable of doing both."

The Indians and their fans didn't have to wait long to find out.

With the whole world watching on Opening Day, April 8, 1975, Robinson hit a home run in his first at-bat to help the Indians to a 5–3 victory over the visiting New York Yankees. Robinson was the second man to bat, and the homer came on a 2–2 pitch. It was the 575th home run in Robinson's 20-year career.

"Any home run is a thrill, but I've got to admit, this one was a bigger thrill," Robinson told reporters after the game.

"Right now," he said, "I feel better than I have after anything I've done in this game. Take all the pennants, the personal awards, the World Series, the All-Star Games together, and this moment is the greatest. The greatest."

The crowd of 56,204 delirious fans who braved the 36-degree temperature roared its approval, prompting Lebovitz to write, "And even if you were frozen, the heart pounded faster and the blood flowed quicker from the thrill." The headline on top of his column asked, "Was it fiction...?"

In fact, the top headline on the front page of *The* (Cleveland) *Plain Dealer* referred to Robinson's storybook debut, and Russell Schneider wrote, "It was the kind of a debut for Robinson that even Hollywood wouldn't dare manufacture."

Like all good Hollywood scripts, there was a secondary storyline that involved Robinson and star pitcher Gaylord Perry, who won the Cy Young Award in 1972. After Robinson was hired, Perry was quoted as saying he'd demand $1 more in salary. Then the two argued in spring training about Perry's attitude. Perry was the Opening Day pitcher, and after he threw the first pitch, he tossed the baseball in the dugout to Robinson as a memento of the historic occasion. After Robinson's home run, Perry led his teammates out to greet Robinson at the plate.

The rest of the season wasn't nearly as dramatic—or as successful. Robinson did write a day-by-day account of the season in a book with Dave Anderson titled *Frank: The First Year.* Russell Schneider also wrote a book, *Frank Robinson: The Making of a Manager.* The two books offered some insights into Robinson's evolution from player to manager.

He was born August 31, 1935, in Silsbee, Texas, near Beaumont, the youngest of 10 children. His parents split up, and Robinson and a couple of siblings moved with their mother to Oakland, California, where Robinson became a star athlete at McClymonds High School. Under Coach (and father figure) George Powles, Robinson blossomed into a star third baseman playing with the likes of Curt Flood and Vada Pinson, along with a tall, lean basketball player by the name of Bill Russell. Robinson was just 17 when he was signed by Cincinnati. He played one year in Ogden, Utah, where he batted .348 with 17 home runs and 83 RBIs, before moving to Tulsa and then Columbia, South Carolina, the next two years. Under the tutelage of Manager Birdie Tebbetts in Cincinnati, Robinson hit .290 with 38 home runs and 83 RBIs and became the 1956 National League Rookie of the Year. In 1961, when he hit .323 with 37 home runs and 124 RBIs and led the Reds to the NL pennant, he was named the NL MVP. He was traded to Baltimore in 1965, and in 1966 he won the

Pro Sports Milestones

First African American Coaches by League

League	Coach	Year
NFL	Fritz Pollard	1922*
NBA	Bill Russell	1966
MLB	Frank Robinson	1975

*Started coaching in the American Professional Football League in 1921.

That Frank Duffy and George Hendrick were the first captains Frank Robinson appointed?

Triple Crown—batting .316 with 49 home runs and 122 RBIs—and was named the AL MVP. He was traded to the Los Angeles Dodgers in 1971 and to the California Angels in 1972. Two years later, the Indians obtained the 11-time All-Star and changed the course of history.

Robinson learned there was more to managing than met the eye. In his book he talked about how cutting a player upset him. He discussed learning how to deal with umpires in the wake of a fine and suspension for pushing Jerry Neudecker during a game in May. He criticized himself for not catching the Minnesota Twins batting out of order in a game later that month. He admitted he'd try anything to get his team out of a slump, including drawing the batting order out of a hat. When things were going bad, he thought about having his wife and children return to California so they wouldn't have to hear what fans were saying. Then he reconsidered because he realized he needed their support.

"More and more I'm realizing that managing doesn't involve just baseball," he wrote.

With the Indians plugging along, Seghi announced Robinson's contract as manager would be renewed. Only a handful of reporters, one photographer, one radio reporter, and one television crew showed up for the press conference, as opposed to the throngs that greeted his initial hiring.

"I like it better this way," Robinson wrote. "I'm just another manager now."

The Indians made a late push by winning 27 of their last 42 games and finished the season 79–80, their best record in seven years.

"I always did what I thought was right, what I thought was best for the team," Robinson said. "I have no regrets, and if I had things to do all over again, I'd do everything the same way. I'm looking forward to the day when people will stop writing, 'Frank Robinson, baseball's

TRIVIA

How did the Indians obtain Frank Robinson as a player?

Answers to the trivia questions are on pages 167–168.

first black manager,' and just write, 'Frank Robinson, manager of the Cleveland Indians.'"

In 1976 the Indians improved to 81–78, the first time they'd finished better than .500 since 1968. But when they got off to a 26–31 start in 1977, Robinson was fired on June 19, becoming the first black manager to be fired—just as he'd predicted when he took the job.

"I'm not upset; disappointed is a better way to say it," he said. "It's almost like they're telling me I failed, and I don't believe I failed in anything."

Indeed, Robinson, who was elected to the Baseball Hall of Fame in 1982, went on to manage the San Francisco Giants, the Baltimore Orioles, the Montreal Expos, and the Washington Nationals. He was named Manager of the Year in 1989, when he led Baltimore to an 87–75 record after the Orioles lost 107 games in 1988.

Mike Hargrove:
The Most Popular Indian?

How popular is Mike Hargrove?

After firing him as manager in 1999, the Indians brought him back as a senior advisor in 2003. In writing about the move, reporter Paul Hoynes of *The* (Cleveland) *Plain Dealer* said the Indians "brought Hargrove home."

Hargrove, who played for the Indians from 1979 to 1985 and managed them to 721 victories and two World Series from 1991 to 1999, won the American League Manager of the Year award in 1995, was named the Indians Man of the Year in 1980 and 1981, and won the Good Guy Award in 1985 and 1991.

As popular as Mike Hargrove was, his wife may have been an even bigger hit with the fans. Sharon Hargrove was a frequent guest speaker with a regular television gig and also contributed a column to the *Indians Ink* monthly magazine, donating any proceeds to charity. She was charming in interviews and cheerfully signed as many autographs as her husband.

In a 1996 interview with *The Plain Dealer,* Sharon Hargrove said, "Mike is very supportive of all these activities. He says when I die, he's going to cremate me and put me in a hubcap so I can just keep going and going."

That the couple should come to love Cleveland, and vice versa, came as quite a shock to both of them. They would never have guessed that when Hargrove was traded to the Indians from San Diego for Paul Dade on June 14, 1979.

"I was devastated," Sharon Hargrove said of the trade in the 1996 interview. "I couldn't imagine living here and playing in that big, empty stadium. It was one of the saddest days of my life."

The Hargroves, high school sweethearts from Perryton, Texas, already had been married nine years by the time Mike Hargrove became an Indian. He took a somewhat unorthodox route to the major leagues, seeing as he never played baseball at Perryton High School, which named its baseball field after him anyway. He played football, basketball, and golf in high school. He was all-state in football in 1968—this is Texas high school football, remember—and was named the outstanding back after intercepting three passes and

Mike Hargrove gives home-plate umpire Joe Brinkman an earful after Brinkman called the first three pitches from Indians pitcher Dwight Gooden balls in Game 2 of the Division Series on September 30, 1998.

By the NUMBERS

Longest Hitting Streaks by Indians

Games	Player	Year
31	Nap Lajoie	1906
30	Sandy Alomar Jr.	1997
29	Bill Bradley	1902
28	Joe Jackson	1911
	Hal Trosky	1936
27	Dale Mitchell	1953
26	Harry Bay	1902
24	Matt Williams	1997
23	Charlie Jamieson	1923
	Tris Speaker	1923
	Dale Mitchell	1951
	Ray Fosse	1970
	Mike Hargrove	1980

throwing for the winning touchdown in a high school All-Star Game in the Greenbelt Bowl. He also was all-conference in basketball. He played football and basketball at Northwest Oklahoma State University, and when the baseball coach invited him to come out for the team, he decided to play baseball, too, becoming an all-conference first baseman in his first season.

By 1972 the 6'0", 195-pound Hargrove was drafted by the Texas Rangers, although he was the 527th player taken in the June draft. He batted .267 in his first season in the minors and almost gave up the game. But he improved to .351 in his second season, and he made his major league debut in 1974. He was the American League Rookie of the Year in 1974 when he batted .323 for the Rangers, and he made the All-Star team the next season when he batted .303. After the 1978 season the Rangers traded him to San Diego, where he got off to a slow start, batting just .192 in 52 games. That's when the Padres sent him to Cleveland, where he wound up batting .325 and starting the love affair that persists to this day.

He played the next six seasons for the Indians, earning the nickname "the Human Rain Delay" for the convoluted routine he performed during each at-bat, adjusting every piece of clothing and grooming the batter's box as well. The routine had to be at least partially responsible for the fact that he led the league with 97 walks in 1976 and 107 in 1978.

Hargrove was cut by the Indians during spring training in 1986, tried to catch on with Oakland, and then decided to retire as a player. But his career as an executive started the same summer, when he was hired as a batting instructor at Batavia in the New York–Penn League. He made his way up the ranks, managing at Kinston in 1987, Williamsport in 1988, and Colorado Springs in 1989, where he was named Manager of the Year for the second time in three years. He joined the Indians as a first-base coach in 1990–91 and replaced John McNamara as manager on July 6, 1991.

TRIVIA

What is Mike Hargrove's real first name?

Answers to the trivia questions are on pages 167–168.

Thus began the team's resurgence that included five straight Central Division titles and World Series appearances in 1995 and 1997. But when the Indians lost a 2–0 lead in the best-of-five division series to the Boston Red Sox in 1999, Hargrove was fired and replaced by Charlie Manuel.

Hargrove was hired by the Baltimore Orioles in 2000 and fired in 2003, at which point he returned to the Indians, until being hired by the Seattle Mariners in 2005. He and his wife still live in the Cleveland area in the off-season.

Super Joe Charboneau

Joe Charboneau came along too early.

The slugging Charboneau burst onto the scene as the 1980 American League Rookie of the Year. But he was known as much for his eccentric behavior as his hitting, and both endeared him to Cleveland fans. Some of his stunts, like drinking beer through his nose or opening a bottle with his eye socket or forearm, would have been perfect for *Late Night with David Letterman*'s "Stupid Human Tricks," but the show didn't premier until 1982.

Told in the summer of 2006 that maybe it wasn't too late to try to get on Letterman, Charboneau laughed and said, "If you want to promote it, go ahead."

The baseball part of his story is woefully short. In 1980 he batted .289 with 23 homers and 87 RBIs for the Indians and led the team in game-winning hits, winning AL Rookie of the Year. This led to an intense round of adulation that included a Super Joe book, songs, and lots of appearances and endorsements.

In a story all too familiar to Indians fans who have heard it again and again—not just about Charboneau, but about many young prospects in the Indians organization—expectations were sky high the next season. But Charboneau hurt his back after sliding head-first into second base during an exhibition game in Tucson. Some doctors thought he'd ruptured a disc, others cleared him to play. He batted .210 in the first half of the season before the players went on strike. He gained 20 pounds during the strike, and shortly after play resumed in August, he was sent down to Triple A Charleston. He had back surgery after the season, then hit .330 in spring training in 1982.

But he batted just .214 in 22 games with the Indians in 1982, spent most of the season in the minors, and was released in 1983.

It was not the career he envisioned, certainly not the career the Indians and their fans craved. But almost 25 years after playing his last game with the Indians, Charboneau is content.

"I'm not bitter," said Charboneau, who remains in the Cleveland area running his hitting school, Unlimited Sports. "Of course, I'm very disappointed. But I'm not bitter. I have some articles from my rookie career that quote me as saying, 'I just hope I stay healthy.' The type of player I was...I didn't have as much talent as most guys, so I tried to play harder. So there was always that possibility [of injury]. That's just part of ball. I'd never gotten hurt until then.

"But if I had to trade five years in the big leagues for Rookie of the Year, I don't think I would. I really wanted it. I'm overall happy. I wish I had a bigger pension. But I think I accomplished about as much as I could with the talent I had."

Despite the shortness of his playing career, Charboneau remains a popular figure in the community and still does promotional work for the team. He did work in the Frontier League as a coach and director of baseball operations in Canton, Ohio. He also coached in Washington, Pennsylvania; Crestwood, Illinois; and Richmond, Indiana. He could see himself returning after taking 2006 off to stay in Cleveland, run his hitting school, and coach 11-year-olds.

One reason he misses the Frontier League: "There's no place I sleep better than on the bus," he said.

That Charboneau has made a comfortable living from baseball was all he could ask. Born June 17, 1955, in Belvidere, Illinois, he grew up in the Santa Clara area. His father left, and his mother was a receptionist at a local hospital. The family was poor and moved a lot. So when Charboneau had a chance to sign with Philadelphia for a $5,000 bonus in 1976, he jumped at it. But after a year in the minors, he quit for a year, then returned in 1978 and batted .350 at Visalia, before being dealt to the Indians for Cardell

TRIVIA

Name the Indians' American League Rookies of the Year, as named by the Baseball Writers Association of America.

Answers to the trivia questions are on pages 167–168.

Joe Charboneau (far right), who still lives in the Cleveland area and remains involved with the team, models the new road-gray jersey that debuted for the 2002 season. Other models include (from left) the team's catcher at the time, Einar Diaz; Coach Joel Skinner; and former pitcher Len Barker.

Camper. In 1979 he set a Double A Southern League record batting .352 at Chattanooga.

His legend started to grow before he reached Cleveland in 1980. There was talk that he could bench-press 400 pounds and do 200 sit-ups. After an exhibition game in Mexico City that spring, the 6'2", 205-pound left fielder was stabbed by a guy with a Bic pen. Though he required medical attention, he wasn't seriously injured and made his major league debut on April 11. He was just 4-for-20 going into Opening Day in Cleveland, but he walked, singled, doubled, and hit a home run to lead the Indians to victory. He was greeted by a standing ovation after the home run, and a love affair was born.

Which came first, the adulation or the eccentricity? Hard to tell which fueled the other.

Some things were undeniably true. He named his daughter Dannon after his favorite yogurt. In spring training in 1982, he dyed

DID YOU KNOW . . . That in his short career, Joe Charboneau became just the third batter to hit a home run into the third deck of the left-field stands at Yankee Stadium? Jimmie Foxx and Frank Howard were the first two to reach it.

his hair bright red, and later that season he shaved his head. But did he really use a pair of pliers to fix a broken nose or pull out a tooth? Did he try to eat a whole egg? A light bulb? A shot glass?

Charboneau said he still gets occasional requests or queries about those things.

"Some of them were true," he said. "Some were embellished. Every sportswriter made up their own. Some of the stuff I never heard of until I read it—eating light bulbs and stuff like that. I don't know where all that came from."

After moving from Cleveland to Buffalo to Scottsdale and back to the Cleveland area, where he now lives in North Ridgeville, Charboneau said people don't often recognize his face anymore. That's fine with him. After surgery on his back (twice), ankle, elbow, and hand, he just tries to go about his business and do a little fishing and golfing.

He has accepted his place in Cleveland baseball history and the fact that baseball will always be part of his life.

"I've tried to get out of it," he said. "I've tried to get away from it. But the more I tried, the more full-circle it came. Now I've quit fighting it."

Len Barker's Perfect Night

Joe Tait is best known in Cleveland as the radio voice of the Cavaliers, but on May 15, 1981, he was working as a television announcer, watching Len Barker mow down one Toronto Blue Jay after another at Cleveland Municipal Stadium.

"I remember it was cold, it was damp, it was dreary...and that was just the stadium," Tait recalled, laughing.

Indeed, only 7,290 fans braved the chill that Friday night to watch the Indians, who were 15–8 coming into the game. That certainly was a good start, but no one had any idea how much better things were about to get.

The shaggy-haired, mustachioed Barker had a 2–1 record entering the game, and he wasted no time against the Blue Jays, establishing his dominance with a 1-2-3 first inning, featuring just seven pitches that resulted in three ground outs.

His fastball had been clocked at better than 96 miles per hour, and Barker relied on that through the first three innings. Of the 28 pitches he threw to retire the first nine batters, 18 were fastballs. But starting in the fourth inning, he went to his curveball.

"The one thing I remember most is that Len Barker's curveball was unbelievable," Tait said. "He had a good fastball, but once he got that curveball going, the Blue Jays were looking for some place to hide. They couldn't handle that. He was on top of his game completely."

He got stronger as the game went on. No batter got as many as three balls against him, and he struck out 11, all swinging, after the third inning. Only five balls made it out of the infield—one to Joe Charboneau in left field and four to Rick Manning in center field, including the final out by Ernie Whitt.

Barker threw a total of 103 pitches, 74 of them strikes. He threw 61 curveballs, 40 fastballs, and two change-ups.

As the game progressed, Tait knew he was watching history. He was just very careful about how he talked about it on the air. At the end of the top of each inning, Tait would say something like, "No runs, no hits, no errors for the Blue Jays," and hope listeners realized what he was saying.

"I'm old school," he explained. "Thou shalt not mention a no-hitter or a perfect game before its time. I'd sooner cut out my tongue."

Barker, of course, never tires of talking about the game.

"Not at all," he told reporters during a 25th anniversary celebration of the game on May 13, 2006, in Jacobs Field. Barker threw out the first pitch to Manning. ("It was a curveball," Barker said with a

Len Barker is mobbed by teammates after pitching a perfect game against the Toronto Blue Jays in Cleveland on May 15, 1981.

Trials and Tribulations

Almost from the start, the Indians have known tragedy.

In 1911 pitcher Addie Joss died from tubercular meningitis two days after his 31st birthday. The native of Woodland, Wisconsin, who attended the University of Wisconsin, had a record of 160–97 with the Naps from 1902 to 1910. He had pitched one perfect game and one no-hitter. In his major league debut, he held the St. Louis Browns to one hit. A sore arm limited him to just 13 games in 1910, but apparently he was thinking of returning when he took ill. He died a short time later.

"The news spread throughout the country like wildfire yesterday, and everywhere Addie was known there was mourning, for a more popular player than Addie never lived," wrote Henry P. Edwards in *The* (Cleveland) *Plain Dealer* on April 15, 1911. "Big in physique, big in mind, and big in heart, he possessed every quality that goes to make the popular man and athlete, and his universal popularity was deserved. No one ever heard Addie knock, and every fan knows ballplayers have plenty of opportunities to do so."

So well thought of was Joss that the Veterans Committee of the Baseball Hall of Fame waived its rule requiring 10 major league seasons, and Joss was inducted in 1978. His career ERA of 1.89 is still the franchise record, as are his 45 shutouts.

It was less than 10 years before the fate struck again. On August 16, 1920, star shortstop Ray Chapman was hit in the head by a pitch thrown by Carl Mays of the New York Yankees at the Polo Grounds in New York.

It was the first pitch from Mays in the top of the fifth inning, and it struck Chapman near the left temple. He collapsed on the spot,

IF ONLY . . . Those two words have probably been said over and over by anyone associated with the 1993 Indians. Undoubtedly, the Olin and Crews families have uttered them time and time again. If only the team hadn't had a day off. If only the weather had been bad. If only somebody, anybody, had talked Steve Olin, Tim Crews, and Bob Ojeda out of going on the boat. How that might have affected that season, or future seasons, is unknown, and frankly unimportant compared to how it would have affected the well-being of their families and teammates.

and umpire Tom Connolly immediately called to the stands for a physician. When Chapman regained consciousness, he was helped to his feet and eventually was able to walk off the field supported between two teammates. However, as he approached the dugout, he seemed to collapse again, according to newspaper accounts. Though he was unable to speak at the time, *The* (Cleveland) *Plain Dealer* reported that he was speaking that night at the hospital.

The *Plain Dealer* of August 17, 1920, reported that Indians manager Tris Speaker was optimistic, despite fears of Chapman having a fractured skull. Of course, the next day the top headline was that Chapman had died and his body was en route to Cleveland. He was the only player ever fatally wounded during a game.

Once again the Indians and baseball mourned a terrific player who was widely respected. In fact, so outraged were members of the American League teams in Boston and Detroit that they started a petition to ban Mays, who had hit 55 batters since joining the league in 1915. Nothing ever came of it.

Chapman, who was 29 when he died, was a native of Beaver Dam, Kentucky. He had a career .278 batting average from 1912 to 1920 with 364 RBIs and 233 stolen bases.

In a copy of his funeral oration kept by the main branch of the Cleveland Public Library, the Reverend Dr. William A. Scullen described Chapman as "ever kind, gentle, courteous, and wholesome...the friend that the soul is ever seeking...

"This was Ray Chapman, respected, admired, honored, loved, not only in this city but in all great cities of America.... The glory was his as a man. It still lives.... To other youths, may it be their fortune to play as fair as he did, may it be their fortune to die as he died, and as we say the last farewell, may the prayer that is in your hearts, the prayer that I trust will be there many times in the future as you remember him be: May the soul of the gentle kindly youth, who Heaven knows, rest in peace."

But the tragic deaths of Joss and Chapman did not prepare the Indians or their fans for March 22, 1993.

As usual, the optimism of spring training was palpable. Popular former Indians player Mike Hargrove had led the team to a 76–86 record and fourth-place finish in his first full season as manager in 1992, and the team seemed poised to turn a corner. In fact, former Los Angeles Dodgers pitchers Tim Crews and Bob Ojeda were so convinced the Indians were up-and-comers that they signed free-agent contracts with Cleveland. Crews would join the bullpen staff led by ace Steve Olin, a submarine-style pitcher who had come up through the Indians farm system and had eight victories and 29 saves in 1992. Ojeda was slated as a number two starter.

On Monday, March 22, the only scheduled off-day during spring training, Crews invited Olin, Ojeda, and their families over for a picnic at the home he was renting on Little Lake Nellie. There was horseback riding and swimming, and that evening the three pitchers decided to go fishing. Around 7:30 PM, they were in Crews's 18-foot bass boat traveling at a high rate of speed when it crashed into an unlit dock. Olin died immediately; Crews died the next morning. Both suffered massive chest and head injuries. Ojeda suffered a severe scalp injury and lost more than two quarts of blood. Tests later showed Crews's blood-alcohol level to be 0.14, over the then-legal limit of 0.10.

Two women were widowed. Six children were left fatherless. A team was devastated, a city crushed. There seemed to be no end to the tears and sadness. Former Indian Andre Thornton, whose wife and daughter were killed in 1977 when the van he was driving flipped on an icy road in Pennsylvania, spoke at the memorial service, talking about the brevity of life.

Slowly, slowly, things started to return to normal, even if they would never be quite the same. Somehow the Indians, including Ojeda, forced themselves to play baseball again. In the end, their 76–86 record left them in sixth place. About a month after the season, Indians pitcher Cliff Young was killed when his car ran into a tree while he reportedly was trying to light a cigarette.

Ten years after the boating accident, then Indians general manager John Hart still called the incident an open wound. Hargrove said he'd never gotten over it. As long as he was manager, the Indians never again had an off-day during spring training.

In addition to all those untimely deaths, the team suffered through catastrophic injuries as well. Pitcher Ray Caldwell was hit by lightning in a game against Philadelphia in 1919. A bolt hit near the mound and the ricochet knocked out Caldwell, who was revived and finished the game.

Divers search for clues near the dock where Indians pitchers Tim Crews and Steve Olin were killed in a boating accident in March 1993. A third pitcher, Bob Ojeda, barely survived.

That former Indians strength coach Fernando Montes actually had been in the boat with Steve Olin, Tim Crews, and Bob Ojeda when they realized they'd forgotten some fishing gear? According to a story by *Plain Dealer* sportswriter Bob Dolgan on the 10th anniversary of the crash, Montes, Olin, and Ojeda played the hand game of Rock, Paper, Scissors to see who would have to get off the boat and retrieve the gear. Montes lost the game, which may have saved his life.

On September 13, 1948, pitcher Don Black suffered a brain hemorrhage. In 1964 Manager Birdie Tebbetts had a near-fatal heart attack at the end of spring training. Later that year, third baseman Max Alvis came down with spinal meningitis. In 1966 shortstop Larry Brown suffered multiple skull fractures and was in a coma after a collision with left fielder Leon Wagner. In 1970 catcher Ray Fosse suffered a separated right shoulder when he was run over by Pete Rose in the All-Star Game. Later that year, Tony Horton suffered a nervous breakdown after being pulled from the lineup by Manager Alvin Dark. In 1983 Manager Mike Ferraro learned he had kidney cancer before the start of spring training. In 2000 Manager Charlie Manuel suffered a ruptured colon during spring training and needed additional surgery during the regular season.

But by far the most infamous injury was suffered by former pitcher Herb Score. The left-hander was voted the 1955 Rookie of the Year when he won 16 games and led the league in strikeouts. He led the league in strikeouts again in 1956, when he won 20 games. On May 7, 1957, in a game at Cleveland Municipal Stadium, he threw a fastball to Gil McDougald of the New York Yankees. McDougald lined the ball back toward the mound, where it struck Score near his right eye. Score collapsed and blood spurted everywhere. He was hospitalized for three weeks, and his season was over. He was never the same, although he blamed a torn tendon in his elbow suffered in 1958. After retiring in 1962, Score was a broadcaster with the Indians from 1964 until 1997.

Wayne Garland's injury was much less dramatic, but its impact on the Indians' future was similar. When free agency was in its infancy, the Indians hoped to make a big splash by signing Garland,

TRIVIA

Where did Bob Ojeda finish his pitching career?

Answers to the trivia questions are on pages 167–168.

whose screwball had helped him go 20–7 with Baltimore in 1976. So they signed the 26-year-old for 10 years at the unheard-of price of $2.3 million in 1977. But on a cold, windy day in Tucson, he hurt his arm warming up for his first spring training game. He tried to pitch through it that day and the rest of the season. He gutted his way to 13 victories and 21 complete games with a 3.59 ERA that season, but he had major shoulder surgery after the season and went 15–29 the next four years and was released after the 1981 season.

It took the Indians more than 10 years to recover.

Albert Belle

Every reporter who covered the Cleveland Indians for any length of time in the early to mid-1990s has an Albert Belle story to tell. Just ask Hannah Storm.

The former NBC broadcaster who has moved to CBS found herself the target of a profanity-laced tirade by Belle in the Indians dugout two hours before the start of Game 3 of the 1995 World Series. Storm was in the dugout to conduct a prearranged interview with Kenny Lofton of the Indians. Despite the verbal assault by Belle, she stood her ground, conducted the interview, and then filed a complaint with Major League Baseball. MLB eventually fined Belle $50,000 for the incident, which cast a pall over the Indians' return to the World Series for the first time in 41 years.

"That 1995 season should have been a celebration, but it wasn't because of him," Paul Hoynes, the longtime baseball writer for *The* (Cleveland) *Plain Dealer,* said, referring to Belle. "He was like Darth Vader."

Hoynes, Sheldon Ocker of the *Akron Beacon Journal,* and Jim Ingraham of the *News-Herald* are the holy trinity of baseball writers. Each has covered the Indians for more than 20 years, a stretch no three beat writers in the country can match. Asking them to relate their favorite Belle stories unleashes a torrent of memories, most of them bad.

However, Ingraham did allow, "I enjoyed covering him as a player, because he was such a great player. But after a few years, it got to be tiresome."

Added Hoynes, "It was a circus. It got to be Albert Belle and the Indians, not just the Indians. Every time we were in New York, we

TOP 10

Indians Single-Season Slugging Percentages

	Name	Slugging Percentage	Year
1.	Albert Belle	.714	1994
2.	Manny Ramirez	.697	2000
3.	Albert Belle	.690	1995
4.	Jim Thome	.677	2002
5.	Manny Ramirez	.663	1999
6.	Hal Trosky	.644	1936
7.	Earl Averill	.627	1936
8.	Jim Thome	.624	2001
9.	Albert Belle	.623	1996
10.	Rocky Colavito	.620	1958

wound up waiting outside the American League president's office because Albert was always getting suspended for something.

"He made your life miserable. You never knew what he was going to do."

That seemed to be the norm once Belle became a public figure. Belle and his twin brother, Terry, were born on August 25, 1966, in Shreveport, Louisiana. Their father was a high school coach. Their mother was a math teacher. Albert Belle, who went by the name of Joey until early in his major league career, was a two-time all-state baseball player at Huntington High School, where he also played football and was a member of the National Honor Society.

When he moved on to Louisiana State University, he was a first-team All-Southeastern Conference selection in 1986 and 1987, when he had a combined .332 batting average and .670 slugging average with 49 home runs and 172 RBIs. Unfortunately, he also exhibited some of the troublesome behavior that overshadowed his career. In 1986 he was involved in a confrontation with a fan in the stands who allegedly made racist remarks, and Belle was suspended from the College World Series.

Still, the Indians drafted him in the second round of the 1987 draft, and two years later he was in the major leagues. By 1993 he made the first of five straight All-Star appearances. In 1994, when his batting average soared to .357, the Chicago White Sox accused him of corking his bat during a game on July 15. The charge proved to be true and netted a 10-game suspension (reduced to seven) in spite of the fact that teammate Jason Grimsley made a heroic, some might say idiotic, attempt to clear Belle. The 6'3", 180-pound Grimsley (whose own baseball career came to a dramatic end in 2006 when he was found with a supply of human growth hormone while pitching for the Arizona Diamondbacks) climbed up through the ceiling tiles in Manager Mike Hargrove's office in Comiskey Park, wriggled through the air ducts to the umpire's room, climbed down, and replaced the confiscated corked bat with one of Paul Sorrento's bats that was uncorked. (Apparently it was impossible to replace one Belle bat with another because all of them were corked.) Although Grimsley was never caught (he revealed his part in the caper in a 1999 article in *The New York Times*), the umpires

Despite on-field success, the star-crossed Albert Belle always seemed to be looking over his shoulder during his days in Cleveland.

discovered the obvious switch because the players' names are printed on their bats. They demanded a return of the original bat, which led to the suspension.

It was one of many suspensions and fines handed out to Belle, none of which seemed to make the least impression. During his time in Cleveland, he threw one baseball at a fan in the stands who was heckling him about his alcohol abuse and rehabilitation, threw another baseball at a photographer, and used his Ford Explorer to chase down some young trick-or-treaters who threw eggs at his house, slightly bumping one of them with his SUV in the process.

For Ingraham, drilling the fan with the baseball in 1991 was a hint of what was to come.

"That was the first inkling we had that his reputation was justified," Ingraham said. "The guy was heckling him from left field in the old stadium. He threw a line drive that hit the guy in the chest. This was in the days before ESPN, so there was no replay of it. It was like, 'Did I just see what I thought I just saw?' We'd heard about his problems in the minor leagues and college, but this was the first tangible evidence this guy was going to be a problem for the team."

Of course, hitting a fan in the chest with a baseball or chasing after trick-or-treaters, one of whom sued Belle, were public actions. Those who covered the team had many private run-ins with Belle, who could turn any day into an adventure.

Here are a few stories that didn't make the papers.

Hoynes: "Albert liked to keep the locker room freezing. One day during the summer, a couple of pitchers, including Eric Plunk, were sitting across from his locker wearing those long coats they wear to keep warm in the bullpen in the early spring and late fall and drinking cups of coffee. He never even looked up. The players would come in between innings and turn up the thermostat, but Albert would come in and turn it back down. Finally, he got tired of the whole thing, set the thermostat to 32 degrees, and smashed it off the wall with his bat. Somebody wrote Mr. Freeze on the wall, and they made the No. 8 on his locker into a snowman."

Ocker: "I remember one spring training we were in Clearwater for a game with the Phillies. An older couple approached the fence behind Albert and said, 'Mr. Belle, could you sign our baseball?'

DID YOU KNOW . . . That Belle became just the fourth player to string together eight straight seasons of 30 home runs and 100 RBIs? The first three? Babe Ruth, Jimmie Foxx, and Lou Gehrig.

Albert just sat there. He wouldn't turn around. The couple kept talking to him, asking him to sign their ball. This went on for three minutes. 'We came all this way just to see you,' they told him. Finally, Albert turned around. 'I guess you came for nothing,' he said. He never did sign the ball or say anything else to them."

Plain Dealer columnist Bill Livingston: "He told me all about his alcohol problem once in an exclusive. He drank 'gorilla farts,' which were, I think, pure-grain alcohol and 151-proof rum, so the whole thing was like 70 percent alcohol. I did a sympathetic piece. This was just after he finished his 12-step program and changed his name to Albert from Joey. The next day, he treated me like he had never met me before."

Plain Dealer columnist Bud Shaw: "I walked into Jacobs Field one day and heard the words no reporter ever wants to hear—'Albert is looking for you.' Seems he took offense to a largely flattering column about the fact that he had become such a student of hitting. Manager Mike Hargrove and Coach Davey Nelson had both told me that Belle kept an exhaustive account of each at-bat on index cards and that he would come up between at-bats to write down the situation, the count, the umpire, what each pitcher threw him, etc. Albert accused me of going through his locker, convinced that was the only way I would know about his index cards. Clearly I had not been anywhere near his locker. No one with a choice in the matter ever went near him or his locker. Obviously, he hadn't read the column. It was totally irrational and so totally Albert. A confrontation followed in which he called me the kind of names heard in the Bada Bing Lounge when somebody questions Tony Soprano's authority. Sandy Alomar broke it up just as I was about to hit Albert's fist with my face. I asked for a meeting with General Manager John Hart, in which I told him he was going to have a serious problem one day if Belle's behavior wasn't addressed with him. I remember pointing out to John that the team would soon be in the postseason

IF ONLY . . . Albert Belle had learned how to control his temper, he almost certainly would have been voted the 1995 American League MVP. Undoubtedly, some writers just couldn't bring themselves to vote for such a volatile personality in spite of his greatness on the field. The hip injury that cut short his career likely will be the reason he is kept out of the Hall of Fame. But, again, voters would have to overlook his personality in order to reward him with baseball's highest honor.

surrounded by national media, including women, and that Belle stood a real chance of embarrassing the organization. John listened, apologized for Belle's antics, and told me he'd like to assure me that talking to Albert would do some good. But, Hart said, he had his doubts given that Albert had previously cursed both owner Dick Jacobs (during negotiations) and American League president Dr. Bobby Brown (after a suspension and while being greeted by Brown at an All-Star Game). It didn't make me feel any better that he had mistreated the AL president and the guy who paid his salary, but I understood I shouldn't wait for an apology from Belle.

"After he left Cleveland, I got an email from his email address asking when I was going to stop 'player hating' and tell the truth—that John Hart had broken up a dynasty. I had been waiting 10 years for the opportunity to turn the tables on Albert and wrote back, 'No comment.' A few days went by. I got a reply that said, 'You got me. You gave me one of my own answers.' I say the email came from his email address because you could never be sure that you weren't hearing from Terry, Albert's twin brother, who often called the office when he didn't like something that was in the paper."

Plain Dealer reporter Burt Graeff: "In March 1997 the *Plain Dealer* sent me to Arizona to do some pre-All-Star stories for the game, which was being played in Cleveland that July. One of the stories was on the White Sox and the Central Division. Albert was with the White Sox at the time. I went to Tucson, where the Sox trained. A couple of hours before a Sox exhibition game, I went to their clubhouse to talk to some players. I decided to take a shot at Albert. I approached him with this question, "Albert, got any time for a writer from Cleveland?" He looked at me, then went ballistic. The clubhouse was nearly full, and he went into a tirade, telling me to get the (bleep) out of there and go back to Winter Haven, where the Indians were. The foul-mouthed tirade went on for several minutes. At one point, he yelled out to everyone in the clubhouse that I was from Cleveland and that no one should talk to me. It got to the point where I almost started laughing. He was sitting next to Frank Thomas. The players eventually left to take batting practice. Thomas stayed behind to get some treatment from the trainers. I asked him if he'd talk and he said he would following the treatment. He came out and we talked for about 45 minutes. He was terrific and shrugged when Albert's name came up. I thanked Thomas for the time he took and told him I didn't know what to expect."

Stories like these, no doubt, are at least part of the reason Belle likely will never receive all the accolades he deserved. In 1995, for example, he led the American League in runs, home runs, slugging percentage, and total bases and shared the RBI lead with Boston's Mo Vaughn. Yet the popular Vaughn was named MVP that season as some voters just couldn't bring themselves to elect the surly Belle, who generally ignored reporters when he wasn't abusive toward them. Many of those same reporters also vote for the Hall of Fame, and Belle's chances of being elected are iffy at best, in spite of his great talent on the field.

TRIVIA

Other than being great hitters, what non-baseball characteristic did Albert Belle and Jim Thome share?

Answers to the trivia questions are on pages 167–168.

After the 1996 season, Belle signed a $55 million free-agent contract with the Chicago White Sox. Upon his first return to Jacobs Field, fans showered him with fake paper money. He responded with a three-run home run and an obscene gesture. In 1999 he signed a free-agent deal with the Baltimore Orioles but was forced into retirement in 2000 with a degenerative hip problem.

In 2006 Belle was jailed in Arizona after being charged with stalking a woman with whom he'd had a five-year relationship.

1995: Return to Glory

The Indians felt they'd been cheated out of a chance to advance to post-season play for the first time in 40 years when a labor dispute shortened the 1994 season to 113 games and canceled the playoffs. The Indians had a 66–47 record and trailed Chicago by one game when Commissioner Bud Selig canceled the rest of the season on August 12.

Though the labor woes forced a late start to the next season, the Indians made up for lost time in 1995, when they roared to a 100–44 record and set a major league record with a 30-game lead in the AL Central Division under Manager Mike Hargrove.

In the new expanded playoff format, they breezed past Boston in three games in the best-of-five AL Division Series and then outlasted Seattle in six games in the best-of-seven AL Championship Series to win their first pennant since 1954. They faced Atlanta in the World Series.

Game 1, Saturday, October 21. At Atlanta 3, Cleveland 2— National League Cy Young Award winner Greg Maddux limited the Indians to two hits and two runs, neither of them earned, in a complete-game victory. Orel Hershiser took the loss, his first in eight postseason decisions. He took himself out of the game in the seventh inning after walking the first two batters.

"I felt I wasn't the right man for the job," Hershiser told reporters after the game. "Every pitch I threw was high and outside. I tried to make adjustments, but nothing was working."

The Indians took a 1–0 lead following an error by Rafael Belliard in the first, but the Braves answered with a solo home run by Fred McGriff in the second and added two more runs in the seventh on a fielder's choice by pinch-hitter Luis Polonia and a suicide squeeze

DID YOU KNOW . . . That when the Indians rallied to win Game 3 in the eleventh inning, 7–6, it was the 29th time that season the Indians won in their last at-bat?

bunt by Belliard, who more than made up for his error. Cleveland got a run back in the ninth, when Kenny Lofton, who singled and stole second, scored on a throwing error by McGriff, but the rally was short-lived.

"That was about as well-pitched a game as I've ever seen," Indians manager Mike Hargrove told reporters after the game. "We've been shut down before, but that was a masterful job of pitching."

Game 2, Sunday, October 22. At Atlanta 4, Cleveland 3—The Indians scored first again, taking a 2–0 lead on a two-run home run by Eddie Murray in the second, but the Braves answered and tied the score in the third. Javy Lopez, behind in the count 0–2, broke the tie with a two-run home run in the sixth inning off Dennis Martinez.

"My game plan was to pitch around Lopez and get to Belliard," Martinez told reporters after the game. "But when I got ahead of him 0–2, the plan changed. I started thinking strikeout."

Game 3, Tuesday, October 24. At Cleveland 7, Atlanta 6—It took four hours and nine minutes, but for Cleveland fans who had been waiting 47 years for a World Series victory, it was worth every minute.

Eddie Murray's run-scoring single in the eleventh inning lifted the Indians to their first World Series victory since October 11, 1948.

Cleveland was cruising along with a 5–3 lead when Atlanta scored three runs in the eighth inning for a 6–5 lead. The Indians tied the score in the bottom of the inning on a run-scoring double by catcher Sandy Alomar.

"We told each other, 'If we're going to lose, we're going to go down fighting,'" Alomar told reporters after the game.

First baseman Herbert Perry, in for Paul Sorrento, robbed Chipper Jones of what would have been a run-scoring single in the ninth to preserve the tie and set the stage for Murray's heroics.

"Herbert made the play of the game," Hargrove told reporters after the game.

Game 4, Wednesday, October 25. Atlanta 5, at Cleveland 2— Atlanta broke a 1–1 tie with three runs in the seventh inning, two of them coming on a single by David Justice. Steve Avery and three relievers held the Indians to just six hits—the third time in four games they had six or fewer.

"It's hard to beat anybody when you only get four or five hits," Hargrove told reporters after the game. "We hit some balls hard in the first two innings, but then he started throwing his change-up. We couldn't get the good part of the bat on the ball after that."

Game 5, Thursday, October 26. At Cleveland 5, Atlanta 4— Hershiser and the Indians fought back and staved off elimination with eight hits to beat Maddux.

"I think I may have overmanaged myself in Game 1," Hershiser told reporters after pitching eight innings in the game. "I put my ego

Jim Thome celebrates after watching his two-run homer clear the fence against the Seattle Mariners during the sixth inning of Game 5 of the ALCS on October 15, 1995.

By the NUMBERS

Indians in the 1995 World Series
.179 batting average
19 runs
35 hits
195 at-bats
7 doubles
1 triple
5 home runs

away and was looking out for the team. Today, I was all player. I was gung-ho. I was going to pitch until they took me out."

Albert Belle hit a two-run home run in the first. When Maddux's next pitch was high and tight to Murray, the Indians' designated hitter took a step toward the mound and yelled at Maddux as both benches emptied, though no punches were thrown. Murray ended up walking and getting picked off first to end the inning. Jim Thome and Manny Ramirez each hit a run-scoring single in the sixth. The Indians added an insurance run in the eighth on a home run by Thome, which allowed them to withstand the Braves' rally in the ninth on a two-run home run by Ryan Klesko.

Game 6, Saturday October 28. At Atlanta 1, Cleveland 0— Tom Glavine held the potent Indians offense to just one hit in eight innings—a bloop single by Tony Peña in the sixth inning. Justice hit a homer in the bottom of that inning for the only run as the Braves won their first World Series since 1957 (when they were still in Milwaukee)—and their first ever in Atlanta. Though Glavine was named the MVP of the World Series, he should have shared the honor with the Braves' other pitchers, who held the Indians to an anemic .179 batting average in the six games, five of which were decided by one run.

"This was a good season," Hargrove told reporters after the game. "The only thing we didn't do this year was win this thing. But we played like champions. I really feel we did."

Two days later, 50,000 fans showed they agreed, piling into downtown Cleveland for a parade and pep rally to celebrate the Indians' performance.

Jim Thome:
Super Slugger

On a cool night in late April 2006, twilight was descending on the city of Cleveland as the Indians prepared to host the Chicago White Sox. Radio announcers Tom Hamilton and Mike Hegan were talking about the return of former Indians slugger Jim Thome.

Thome spurned the Indians after the 2002 season when the Philadelphia Phillies offered him a six-year, $85 million contract. It was longer and richer than the deal offered by the Indians. So in spite of his stated love for Cleveland, Thome left for Philadelphia. After the 2005 season, the Phillies traded him to the White Sox, so this was going to be his first game in Jacobs Field since leaving.

Speaking to reporters before the game, Thome, who had been besieged for autographs by fans who had arrived early, said he wasn't sure what kind of reception he would get.

"No matter the reception, I have a lot of great memories from playing here," he said.

But Hamilton and Hegan clearly were worried that Thome was going to get booed. Leading up to the start of the game, they talked about all the reasons why fans should not boo Thome.

He was such a good guy, they said. Given the current state of free agency in baseball, no one spends their whole career in one place anymore, they pointed out.

The talk continued into the top of the first inning, and it was still going on as Thome, the designated hitter who was batting third, walked from the dugout for his first at-bat.

Despite the best efforts of Hamilton and Hegan, the booing from the crowd of 17,845 could be heard over the voices of the announcers.

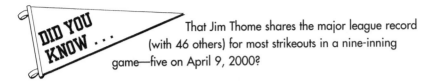

DID YOU KNOW . . . That Jim Thome shares the major league record (with 46 others) for most strikeouts in a nine-inning game—five on April 9, 2000?

Then, in a sort of backlash, came cheers of thanks for what Thome meant to the Indians during some of their most exciting years.

When he struck out swinging, there were more cheers, derisive ones, this time.

The irony is that although Thome switched teams, he never really left Cleveland. He still lives in the area with his wife, Andrea, a former Cleveland television personality, and their daughter, Lila Grace.

"People have been great," he said. "It's definitely kept us here. If it was bad, we'd have never come back."

Thome and Cleveland were a perfect fit. The native of Peoria, Illinois, was the kind of hardworking regular guy made to play in a blue-collar, lunch-bucket-carrying town like Cleveland.

Thome was born on August 27, 1970, three minutes after his twin sister, Jennifer. He was a 1988 graduate of Limestone (Illinois) High School, where he was all-state in baseball and basketball. He played both sports at Illinois Central and was an honorable mention junior college All-American in baseball.

He was drafted by the Indians in the 13th round of the 1989 amateur draft and made his major league debut on September 4, 1991, going 2-for-4 with an RBI. It was 1994 when he played his first full season in the majors. He was strictly a third baseman at that point, but the Indians used him at third base and as a designated hitter in 1995 and 1996. In 1996 he hit .311 with 38 home runs and 116 RBIs. That was good enough to earn him a Silver Slugger award as the best-hitting third baseman in the American League. He also finished 15th in voting for the AL MVP.

The next season the Indians moved him to first base. He responded with a .286 batting average, 40 home runs, and a league-leading 120 walks. He earned the first of three straight AL All-Star berths and finished sixth in the MVP voting.

Thome was drafted by the Indians in the 13th round of the 1989 amateur draft, and his blue-collar work ethic captured fans' hearts in the 1990s.

From then on, the 6'4", 245-pound Thome became one of the most feared hitters in the American League on one of the league's best teams. He was always among the league leaders in on-base percentage. Twice more he led the league in walks (with 127 in 1999 and 122 in 2002) and was second in home runs with 49 in 2001 and 52 in 2002. He also led the league with a .677 slugging percentage in 2002.

One of his most memorable performances came in the 1999 AL Division Series against Boston, when he had four home runs and 10 RBIs. That gave him 16 home runs in postseason play, moving him ahead of Babe Ruth into third place in major league history, behind only Reggie Jackson and Mickey Mantle, with 18 apiece.

TRIVIA

What is Jim Thome's middle name?

Answers to the trivia questions are on pages 167–168.

"Look, I am a guy from Peoria, Illinois," Thome told reporters after he hit his 14th postseason home run, a grand slam off John Wadsin in the fourth inning of Game 2, becoming the first player to hit two grand slams in his postseason career. "Never, ever, growing up as a kid, did I think my name would someday be mentioned in the same sentence with guys like Babe Ruth, Mickey Mantle, or Reggie Jackson."

Thome later moved within one of Jackson and Mantle with another home run in the 2001 AL Division Series against Seattle.

But in addition to all those towering home runs, all those timely walks, it must be noted that Thome remained a down-to-earth, likeable guy—always ready with an autograph or an interview. Some think his willingness to sign all those autographs stems from being snubbed by Dave Kingman when Thome was a young Cubs fan in search of a signature.

He also supported numerous charitable projects and won the 2002 Roberto Clemente Award from Major League Baseball for his community service.

That proved to be his last season in Cleveland. Although Cleveland fans don't want to hear it, it was a gut-wrenching decision for Thome to leave and sign with the Philadelphia Phillies. But the Phillies were offering Thome a six-year, $85 million contract, twice as much money as the Indians.

"When somebody is going to pay you that amount of money, it's hard to turn down," Thome said the night of his return to Cleveland.

Some thought the small-town Thome would struggle in a tough city like Philadelphia.

"You hear the horror stories, but it's really not that bad a place," he said that night in Cleveland. "Playing there, you learn to not let a lot of things bother you."

Of course, how much could have bothered him when he tied Alex Rodriguez for the major league lead in home runs with 47 in 2003? It was the first time a Philadelphia player led the National League in home runs since Mike Schmidt hit 37 in 1986. Thome finished fourth in the NL MVP voting, the highest finish for a Phillie since Lenny Dykstra finished second to Pittsburgh's Barry Bonds in 1993.

His numbers dipped a tad in 2004, when he hit 42 home runs with 105 RBIs, but he still earned his first NL All-Star berth.

In 2005 he was plagued by back and elbow problems, which limited him to a career-low 59 games. Still, in a survey of players by the Tribune Company, Thome was named the best teammate in major league baseball.

No wonder his Chicago teammates, as well as the Cleveland announcers, were so upset with the reaction he received upon his return to Cleveland.

Thome got the last word, however, when he was named the 2006 AL Comeback Player of the Year.

1997: Return Engagement

"Wait 'til next year" is more than just a cliché in Cleveland. It's a way of life.

After their disappointing loss to the Atlanta Braves in six games in the 1995 World Series, the Indians wanted nothing more than a chance to get back and try for another world championship.

Despite winning a league-leading 99 games in 1996, they came up short in the playoffs, losing to the wild-card Baltimore Orioles in four games in the AL Division Series.

They had a good season in 1997, winning 86 games, but the other three American League teams in the playoffs won more, led by Baltimore's 98 victories, New York's 96, and Seattle's 90. However, the Indians beat the defending-champion Yankees in five games in the AL Division Series, with rookie Jaret Wright winning two of those games, and upset the Orioles in six games in the AL Championship Series to get yet another chance to bring a World Series title to Cleveland for the first time since 1948.

Game 1, Saturday, October 18. At Florida 7, Cleveland 4— The Indians lost Game 1. So what else is new? It was the sixth straight time the team had lost the opening game of a playoff series. Moises Alou hit a three-run home run and Charles Johnson followed with a solo shot in the fourth inning off Orel Hershiser, and the Marlins added two runs in the fifth inning.

"There's no defense for what Moises and Charles did," Florida manager Jim Leyland told reporters after the game. "We broke the game open at the right time. At least as far as you can break it open against a team like Cleveland."

Game 2, Sunday, October 19. Cleveland 6, at Florida 1—The Indians scored three times in the fifth inning on a run-scoring single by Marquis Grissom and a two-run single by Bip Roberts with two out. They added a pair of runs on a home run by Sandy Alomar Jr. in the sixth inning en route to winning their first World Series road game since 1948.

"Alomar had a big blow," Leyland told reporters after the game. "We felt we were right in the game at 4–1, but his homer hurt."

Chad Ogea was especially thankful for the offensive output. The Indians had failed to score in his previous 19 innings of postseason baseball.

"These things go in stages," Ogea told reporters after the game. "Sometimes you pitch good and you don't get any runs. Sometimes you pitch bad and you get a lot of runs."

Game 3, Tuesday, October 21. Florida 14, at Cleveland 11—The Marlins scored seven times in the ninth inning to tie one World Series record, and the Indians made three errors in the inning to tie another. The game took four hours and 12 minutes, making it the second-longest nine-inning World Series game in history. It also was the second-highest-scoring game in World Series history. The Indians built a 7–3 lead after five innings, but the Marlins scored twice in the sixth and twice in the seventh to tie the score.

Reliever Eric Plunk gave up four runs on two hits and two walks while retiring just two batters. After the Marlins' outburst in the top of the ninth, the Indians answered with four runs in the bottom of the ninth on a sacrifice fly by Tony Fernandez, a single by Grissom, and a two-run double by Roberts.

"We didn't get good starting pitching, good middle relief, or good short relief," Manager Mike Hargrove told reporters after the game. "I was really surprised with the way our bullpen pitched. That's the one thing our pitching has done all postseason. It's kept us in the ballgame.

"We played so poorly and it was such an ugly game that I don't think we'll have trouble letting this game go."

Game 4, Wednesday, October 22. At Cleveland 10, Florida 3—This time the Indians jumped in front and stayed there to even

That the Indians' 1997 Game 7 World Series loss came on Manager Mike Hargrove's 48th birthday?

the Series. They scored three times in the first inning, when Manny Ramirez hit a two-run home run, and added three runs in the third.

Game 5, Thursday, October 23. Florida 8, at Cleveland 7— Hershiser was victimized by Alou again. This time Alou hit a three-run home run with two out in the sixth inning to rally the Marlins to a 6–4 lead. Florida added single runs in the eighth and ninth. The Indians put three on the board in the bottom of the ninth but still came up short.

"I pitched okay in the early innings, but I didn't execute the pitch to Alou," Hershiser told reporters after the game. "I made another mistake against him."

Said Hargrove to reporters after the game, "Our team has faced a lot of adversity throughout the year and in the postseason, and we've played hard when we've had to."

Game 6, Saturday, October 25. Cleveland 4, at Florida 1— Chad Ogea held the Marlins to one run in five innings and helped his cause with a double and two RBIs off ace pitcher Kevin Brown. Ogea became the first Indians player since Bob Lemon in 1948 to win two World Series games.

"I was just trying to make contact, and the balls happened to go through," Ogea told reporters after the game. "It was fun.... Hitters are going to laugh at me."

While Ogea, who'd had five knee surgeries, nearly passed out after running the bases in the fifth inning, Mike Hargrove almost needed medical attention after watching a stellar play by Omar Vizquel, who dove to his right to stop a ball hit by Charles Johnson and threw him out to save two runs from scoring in the sixth.

"It was the most important play of my career so far," Vizquel told reporters after the game.

"I was getting a drink when Johnson hit the ball, and when Omar dived and stopped it, I almost choked," Hargrove told reporters after the game. "Nothing he does surprises me. He has the guts of a burglar."

Game 7, Sunday, October 26. At Florida 3, Cleveland 2— Behind a super pitching job by Wright, who held the Marlins to two hits and one earned run in six and one-third innings, the Indians were poised to end their 49-year championship drought. A two-out single by Tony Fernandez scored two runs in the third inning and the Indians seemed to be in control. Florida got a run back in the

The Tribe confers on the mound during the eleventh inning of Game 7 of the World Series against the Florida Marlins on October 26, 1997.

seventh, but Cleveland was still leading, 2–1, when its star reliever Jose Mesa took the mound in the ninth inning. After a single by Alou, Mesa struck out Bobby Bonilla, but Johnson's single sent Alou to third, and a sacrifice fly by Craig Counsell scored Alou and tied the game.

TRIVIA

If the 1997 Game 3 was the second-highest-scoring game in World Series history, what was the highest-scoring game in World Series history?

Answers to the trivia questions are on pages 167–168.

Edgar Renteria's two-out RBI single in the eleventh inning off Charles Nagy scored the winning run as the Marlins won their first World Series title in just their fifth year of existence.

"I can't tell you how disappointed I am," Hargrove told reporters after the game. "You only get these chances so many times. But I'm proud of my players. No one gave us a chance to be here.... I wish I had a nickel for every time I heard somebody say that we played in a weak division or called us underachievers. I'm proud of the way we played this year."

A Gold Glove Personality

One of the things that made Omar Vizquel so popular with fans and reporters was that he was involved with so many things outside of baseball. His wide range of interests, combined with his friendly and outgoing personality, drew people to him, and those who approached him were rarely disappointed.

He could discuss the latest trends in food, fashion, or music. He could laugh at himself.

When he got off to a particularly hot start in 2002, batting .311 into June with eight home runs and a .513 slugging percentage, reporters teased him that he might start getting questions about steroid use.

"That would be awesome if they asked me about that, a little guy like me," said Vizquel, 5'9" and 185 pounds.

Even when he wasn't particularly interested in a certain subject, he was still worth interviewing. Before the presidential election in 2004, Vizquel was asked how politically active he and his teammates were.

"It's not a subject you hear [discussed in the locker room] very often," said Vizquel, who became a U.S. citizen in 2004. "Guys are more concerned about things happening around their environment, which is sports. We watch ESPN, not CNN."

With that kind of facility with the language, it was no surprise that when he decided to write his autobiography with *Akron Beacon Journal* writer Bob Dyer in 2002, books went flying off the shelves.

Of course, the fact that he called out former teammate Jose Mesa in the very first chapter had something to do with that, too.

Cleveland fans have never forgiven Mesa, the Indians' former ace reliever, for giving up the tying run to the Florida Marlins in the bottom of the ninth inning of Game 7 of the 1997 World Series. The Indians went into that ninth inning leading 2–1 and were two outs away from their first World Series title since 1948. The Marlins went on to win in the eleventh inning.

Chapter 1 of Vizquel's book is titled "Game Seven."

Writes Vizquel, "The most important asset for a major league baseball player is not speed or size or strength. It's mental toughness.

"I pride myself on being strong between the ears. At this level of competition, 80 percent of the game is psychological. Unless you

Omar Vizquel leaps over Toronto runner Paul Molitor during a double-play attempt on August 30, 1995.

IF ONLY . . . Reliever Jose Mesa had retired Moises Alou and Charles Johnson or Craig Counsell, or any two of the three—a thought that probably occurs to the truest Indians fans on a daily basis—in Game 7 of the 1997 Series, the Indians would have been celebrating their first World Series title since 1948. Of course, Vizquel would have had to come up with a different beginning to his autobiography, but that probably wouldn't have been a problem.

have absolute faith in your ability, it doesn't matter how fast you can run or how hard you can throw.

"That's why I was worried when I went to the mound in the ninth inning of Game Seven of the 1997 World Series.

"Jose Mesa, our ace relief pitcher, had come in to try to protect a one-run lead. All we had to do was get three outs and we'd win the ultimate title. The eyes of the world were focused on every move we made. Unfortunately, Jose's own eyes were vacant. Completely empty. Nobody home. You could almost see right through him.

"Jose's first pitch bounced five feet in front of the plate. And, as every Cleveland Indian fan knows, things got worse from there."

Well, then. No one could argue with the facts. It's just that baseball players usually go to great lengths to cover for each other. Much more common in that situation would be for one player to say, "Well, we should never have let it come down to one run in the ninth inning." Or, "We had our chances to score in extra innings."

But Vizquel told it like it was for millions of hurting Indians fans.

Not surprisingly, Mesa didn't take it too well. In fact, he vowed to hit Vizquel with a pitch every time he faced him. Major League Baseball even suspended him for four games after one such hit.

That only made Mesa more of a villain, and Vizquel more of a hero, in the eyes of Indians fans.

Vizquel's arrival in Cleveland coincided with one of the more exciting—if not ultimately successful—stretches in Indians history. On his first Opening Day in Cleveland, the Indians christened their jewel of a new ballpark, Jacobs Field. Although labor troubles canceled the end of that season, the Indians qualified for the playoffs the next five years and six times in a seven-year stretch. Vizquel brought one Gold Glove with him and won eight more with the Indians. Plus, during his tenure the Indians set a major league record with 455 sell-outs at Jacobs Field (capacity 43,405).

Is it any wonder that he is so closely tied with the team's most recent glory years?

Before becoming a fixture at shortstop with the Indians, Vizquel had become something of a baseball nomad. He grew up in a middle-class household in Caracas, Venezuela. His father was an electrician and his mother stayed home to raise three children. There is no question his family, including wife Nicole and son Nico, is the most important thing in his life.

In the dedication of his book, he wrote, "To my mom, whose love and dedication for her kids made us what we are. To my dad, who practiced baseball with us even when he came home from work exhausted. To my sister, Gabriela, whose smile and love for kids makes me remember how beautiful life is every day. To my brother, Carlos, who has always been next to me, on the field and off, my best double-play partner ever. To my wife, Nicole, who stuck with me through the hard times, who gave me the best gift I ever got—my son—and whose understanding of life and appreciation for another culture is part of her beauty. And to my son, Nico, who is the brightest light in my life and the reason I understand, finally, why my parents took such great care of me when I was young."

Like most kids in Venezuela, Vizquel wanted to be a shortstop like national heroes Davey Concepción and Luis Aparicio. He got his first glove when he was five years old and slept with it. He was only 16 when he signed with the Seattle Mariners as a non-drafted free agent on April 1, 1984, and he had just turned 17 when he reported to Butte, Montana, later that year. Subsequent seasons saw him play in Bellingham, Washington; Wausau, Wisconsin; Salinas, California; Burlington, Vermont; and Calgary, Alberta.

He made his major league debut on April 3, 1989, in Oakland against the Athletics, featuring the Bash Brothers—Jose Canseco and Mark McGwire. Unfortunately, Vizquel's throwing error on a routine grounder by Canseco set the stage for a two-run home run by McGwire as the Mariners lost, 3–2. But the Mariners stuck with him and Vizquel matured and improved. His best season in Seattle was 1992, when he batted .294 and had a .989 fielding percentage. He hit

By the
NUMBERS

Omar Vizquel's Fielding Percentage by Year
during His Tenure with the Indians

Year	Fielding Percentage
1994	.981
1995	.986
1996	.971
1997	.985
1998	.993
1999	.976
2000	.995
2001	.989
2002	.990
2003	.978
2004	.982

.255 and had a .980 fielding percentage with 15 errors in 1993, and that December he was traded to Cleveland for shortstop Felix Fermin, first baseman Reggie Jefferson, and cash.

It proved to be a great deal for Vizquel and for the Indians. Not only did he and they enjoy some of their finest seasons on the field— Vizquel, master of the barehanded catch, was named to the All-Star team in 1998, 1999, and 2002—but Vizquel made his presence felt in the community as well. In 1996 he won the Hutch Award, named for former pitcher and manager Fred Hutchinson. It is presented annually to the major league player who best exemplifies character, desire, and fighting spirit. In 1998 he was nominated for the Roberto Clemente Award, which goes to a great player who is active in community service.

It was no surprise then that when Vizquel became a free agent after the 2004 season that the Cleveland community hoped and prayed the Indians would re-sign him. But his age (37) was working against him and the budget-conscious Indians had other priorities, as well as some promising young shortstops in their farm system. Even so, almost everybody in the organization—and the city—was sad when Vizquel signed a three-year, $12.25 million contract with the San Francisco Giants on November 16, 2004.

The Indians and the Arts

It may not rival *Pride of the Yankees* or *Bang the Drum Slowly* for drama, and it may not come close to *The Natural* for beautiful cinematography, but for plain old fun in the movie theater, it's hard to beat *Major League.*

The 1989 comedy about the Cleveland baseball team, starring Tom Berenger, Charlie Sheen, and real-life baseball broadcaster Bob Uecker, was a huge hit—not just in Cleveland, but around the world. The fact that it was not actually filmed in Cleveland's Municipal Stadium did nothing to diminish its popularity with Indians fans, who hoped against hope that their team, like the fictitious one in the movie, would one day triumph again.

It wasn't the first movie made about the team. *The Kid from Cleveland* was a 1949 film about the Indians going to bat for a troubled teenager. Indians owner Bill Veeck, manager Lou Boudreau, pitcher Bob Feller, and former Indians Tris Speaker and Satchel Paige all appeared in the film.

Since then, the Indians have been well represented in the arts. They have been featured in numerous movies and books. Some have been serious musicians. Others dabbled in art. In fact, Lissa Bockrath, wife of General Manager Mark Shapiro, is an accomplished artist whose specialty is oil paint on photographs of the urban landscape.

One former Indian, John Berardino, actually became much better known as an actor. A utility infielder on the Indians' 1948 team that won the World Series (though he didn't actually play in the fall classic), Berardino became famous as the beloved patriarch Dr. Steve Hardy on the daytime soap opera *General Hospital* from 1963 until his death in 1996.

Former shortstop Omar Vizquel was an artist on and off the field. His barehanded catches became almost routine. But away from the diamond, he was a man of many other talents. He went to Seattle Academy of Art and studied oil painting, becoming an accomplished artist. A fan of Salvador Dalí and Peter Max, he also became an art collector. Long before it became fashionable, he used a digital camera to create art on his laptop and also created his own website. He has done stand-up comedy, trying some of it out on the huge crowd in Public Square that celebrated the 1995 season after the Indians lost to the Atlanta Braves. He started playing timbale (kettledrums) because he loved salsa music and then moved to regular drums, making his on-stage debut in September 1999, with fellow Indians Jim Thome, Dave Burba, Richie Sexson, and Mark Langston with Michael Stanley. He has designed his own clothing line and created his own salsa and ice cream.

Other players who were musically inclined included pitcher Jack "Black Jack" McDowell, outfielder Coco Crisp, and first baseman Ben Broussard. McDowell is a guitarist with Stickfigure. His former band, V.I.E.W., opened for the Smithereens in 1992. Crisp wrote a rap song, "We Got That Thing," featured on a 2005 CD titled *Oh, Say Can You Sing* that featured 10 other baseball players, including Hall of Famer Ozzie Smith. Broussard also plays the guitar and writes songs and put out a solo acoustic rock CD in 2005 titled *Ben Broussard*. He performed selections from the CD at a concert at Cleveland's House of Blues.

But movies and books are, by far, the most popular vehicles for the Indians' entry into the world of the arts. In addition to the two movies about the Indians, numerous players have had chances to act on—or at least appear on—the big screen. Joe Charboneau, for instance, had a bit role in *The Natural* in 1984.

The following list was accumulated by author Marc Davis in *Cleveland Indians Facts & Trivia*:

In 1949 Gene Bearden played himself in *The Stratton Story* about Chicago White Sox pitcher Monty Stratton. The movie starred Jimmy Stewart.

Cleveland Indians catcher Tim Laker (left) sits with Omar Vizquel in their locker room before a game on May 5, 2004, at Jacobs Field. In a scene reminiscent of the movie Major League, *Laker sacrificed the glove Vizquel wore while committing six errors in the first 24 games. Laker built the elaborate altar next to Vizquel's locker and included a bottle of cheap wine, a hanging roasted chicken, a Buddha-like figure, candles, and a baseball with "the curse is killed" written on it.* Photo courtesy of AP via The Plain Dealer, Chuck Crow.

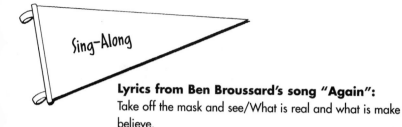

Sing-Along

Lyrics from Ben Broussard's song "Again":
Take off the mask and see/What is real and what is make believe.

Lyrics from "Take It All Back":
Roller coaster up and down/Since we met my feet haven't touched the ground

In 1953 Bob Lemon played St. Louis Cardinals pitcher Jesse Haines in *The Winning Team* with Ronald Reagan as Grover Cleveland Alexander.

In 1959 Paige was Sergeant Sutton in *The Wonderful Country* with Robert Mitchum.

In 1980 Michael Douglas starred as a retired Indian in *It's My Turn* with Bob Feller.

Former Indian Leon Wagner appeared in *A Woman under the Influence* in 1974 and *The Bingo Long Traveling All-Stars and Motor Kings* in 1976.

But none of those seems to have the appeal of *Major League.*

Written and directed by longtime Indians fan David Ward, it told the unlikely story of a team of misfits that banded together and beat the powerful New York Yankees for the American League East title on the last day of the regular season. The new owner of the team, who inherited it from her deceased husband, hates Cleveland and wants to move the team to Miami. But her only way out of the current lease is poor attendance. She puts together the worst team she can, only to have the players find out about her scheme and band together to win.

The movie, which opened the 1989 Cleveland Film Festival, came out before the Indians' most recent rise, so Ward struck the perfect chord with Indians fans desperate for victory. In fact, when the Indians made the 1995 World Series, Ward and several of the actors planned a field trip to Cleveland for one of the games.

In spite of the fact that Pluto was now spending almost every day with his father's favorite team, there was still tension between the two. Baseball players in the 1970s weren't what baseball players in the 1940s and 1950s had been. They were stars now, making a lot of money, instead of regular guys playing for regular salaries and the love of the game.

After five years covering baseball, Pluto covered the NBA's Cleveland Cavaliers for the *Plain Dealer* and then became a columnist in Akron. His career took off, but he had some personal regrets. He never took his dad to spring training. Even though he knew his dad wanted to go to a game in the Indians' final year in Cleveland Municipal stadium in 1993, he never found time to take him.

Then his father suffered a stroke. For more than four years, Pluto, whose mother had died years earlier, traveled from Ohio to Sarasota, Florida, to help his brother care for their dad. During that time, Pluto wrote a few columns about his dad. The first one had to do with not taking him to the stadium in 1993.

"It was a bittersweet thing," Pluto said.

The letters poured in from readers who had similar experiences and similar regrets. They were readers also tethered to their parents—mostly fathers—by a love for baseball.

Eventually, a few columns blossomed into a book, *Our Tribe, A Baseball Memoir,* which is as much about Pluto's father and their relationship as it is about the Indians.

Wrote Pluto of going to the old stadium as a boy with his dad, "I don't remember much about the games or even the players; I just remember being with my father, his arm around me, a Tribe cap on my head."

The book was published in 1999, after Pluto's father died and was buried wearing a Tribe jacket and sweatpants, with a baseball cap in his right hand and a copy of *The Curse of Rocky Colavito* in his left. In the dedication to *Our Tribe,* Pluto wrote, "To my father, Tom Pluto—A REAL TRIBE FAN."

"It was therapeutic," Pluto said of writing the book. "I was writing it while my dad was dying and I was taking care of him. In the last year of his life, he really had problems sleeping. He had congestive heart failure, and his lungs would fill up. I remember sitting at

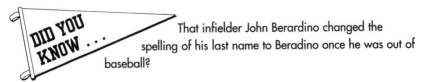

his table in Florida, which was about 30 feet from his bed, working on this while trying to get him to sleep."

During those years he was caring for his father, Pluto came to an understanding of why senior citizens have such a love for the game.

"The thing that makes baseball so hard to cover—the daily grind—is what makes it so appealing to older people," said Pluto, whose favorite baseball book is *False Spring* by Pat Jordan. "It's daily. It's something they can count on.... They can see the players, see their faces. They're normal size, not like football or basketball players.... When they talk about the old players, they become a whole second set of relatives you've never met. You talk about them as much as Aunt Pat and Uncle Myron."

Asked why baseball seems to generate so much more beautiful literature than any other sport, Pluto said, "It's older. The sense of history is much deeper. It started before the turn of the century. The other sports are really post–World War II. You can see more of what's going on in baseball than other sports. It stops and starts. Football stops and starts, but you still don't know what nine of 11 players are doing on any given play. Baseball really is easier to understand. It's easier to write because it's so compartmentalized. It's a very neat and orderly game. The same things that make it boring to watch sometimes make it easy to write [about]. There's so little action and then where there finally is something—it's dramatic.

"Also, the whole romance of riding the buses in the minor leagues with their $4 meal money a day or whatever it is. That does not exist in any other sport. That opens up a whole new avenue of writing. Plus, you have the people from the most parts of the world playing."

All that may be true, but the reason *Our Tribe* is so popular is the realism and genuine emotion depicted in the sort of writing that prompted the *Chicago Tribune* to call Pluto "perhaps the best American writer of sports books."

An example:

"Baseball filled those long, lonely nights when there was just the two of us, and when we really had little to say to each other. Baseball was a medicine when his legs hurt, his chest ached, and depression was gnawing away at the edges of his heart. For the four-plus years after my father's stroke, baseball helped hold us together."

Surely, a tear came to many an eye when Pluto wrote, "I'll always be grateful that baseball could make him happy when he had little else to smile about."

Baseball books and movies can elicit a wide range of reactions...just like the teams that serve as their subjects. From the hilarity of *Major League* to the poignancy of *Our Tribe,* the Indians have captured the imagination of the young and the old, in the ballpark and away from the field.

Looking to the Future

Since the Indians' trip to the World Series in 1997, many things have changed.

Oh, the winning continued. The visits to the postseason continued, for a while anyway.

Cleveland won its fourth straight American League Central Division crown with an 89–73 record in 1998, beat the Boston Red Sox three games to one in the best-of-five AL Division Series, and then lost to the New York Yankees four games to two in the best-of-seven AL Championship Series.

The next season brought more of the same—a 97–65 record, another Central Division crown. Second baseman Roberto Alomar joined his brother Sandy and the cast of Jim Thome, Manny Ramirez, Omar Vizquel, and Bartolo Colon. But although the Indians won the first two games at home, they ultimately lost the best-of-five division series to Boston three games to two, prompting changes.

First, Manager Mike Hargrove was fired. The popular ex-player had the second-most victories of any Indians manager (721) and the third-highest winning percentage (.550). Inevitably, though, the manager pays the price when a team fails to achieve its potential. He was replaced by Charlie Manuel.

Vizquel played for Hargrove six seasons—longer than he'd played for any other manager in the big leagues—and considered him a friend.

"Still, I didn't necessarily disagree with the decision to fire Hargorve after the 1999 season," Vizquel wrote in his 2002 autobiography, *Omar! My Life On and Off the Field.* "It was probably time for him to go. After a while, a manager loses his effectiveness. Players just get tired of hearing him and tune him out. It's not like he did a bad job managing that last year, but I think we probably needed a change."

More changes were coming. The biggest involved the sale of the franchise from Richard E. Jacobs to Lawrence Dolan and family for $323 million. The Dolans assumed ownership on February 15, 2000. In addition, General Manager John Hart, the architect of the great Indians teams of the 1990s, left on October 31, 2001, replaced by the man he groomed as his successor, Mark Shapiro.

Shapiro, son of the agent Ron Shapiro, joined the Indians' baseball operations department in 1992, became assistant director of minor league operations in 1993, director of minor league operations in 1994, and vice president of baseball operations/assistant general manager in 1999. He was promoted to general manager upon Hart's

Center fielder Grady Sizemore has made his spectacular play seem almost routine, and he will serve as a cornerstone for the Indians for years to come.

16—Number of owners that the Cleveland Indians have had.

1900–16 Charles W. Somers

1916–22 Jim Dunn

1922–27 Estate of Jim Dunn

1927–46 Alva Bradley

1946–49 Bill Veeck

1949–52 Ellis Ryan (President)

1953–56 Myron H. "Mike" Wilson (President)

1956–62 William R. Daley

1963–66 Gabe Paul

1967–72 Vernon Stouffer

1972–76 Nick Mileti (President)

1977–78 Ted Bonda (President)

1979–83 F.J. "Steve" O'Neill

1983–86 Estate of F.J. "Steve" O'Neill

1986–2000 Richard E. Jacobs

2000–present Lawrence Dolan and family trusts

departure, and the rebuilding of the team began within a year when he traded Colon to Montreal for Cliff Lee, Grady Sizemore, and Brandon Phillips in the middle of the 2002 season.

Things had been different under Jacobs and Hart. The promising young players on those teams were signed to multiyear contracts when their window to win was wide-open. Jacobs Field was brand-new and the Cleveland Browns football team had moved to Baltimore, leaving sports fans with some disposable income from 1996 to 1998. If Jacobs and Hart thought one more high-priced veteran would put them over the top, they signed him, knowing they had the full support of the fans who would fill Jacobs Field for 455 straight games from 1995 to 2001. They weren't concerned about the team's minor league system. They were designed to win now.

But when they didn't win the ultimate prize after reaching the World Series in 1995 and 1997, something had to give. Those talented veterans, whose expensive contracts were now shorter, were still desirable to teams who needed a quick fix. Because he had come up through the ranks, Shapiro knew the Indians had some work to do to restock their minor league system. After all, in 1999, the Indians ranked 16th in the major leagues in minor league expenditures. Shapiro also knew trading some of the team's aging stars, or not re-signing those who became free agents, would allow him to acquire exactly the kind of young talent that would return the team to greatness—hopefully—in a few years.

It was going to be a tough sell to fans in the short term. After all, Manuel had the Indians back in the playoffs in 2001 after missing the postseason in 2000. The 2001 team took a two-games-to-one lead against Seattle, which won 116 games in the regular season, before falling in five games in the best-of-five AL Division Series. Hart had seen a major rebuilding project was in order, and he didn't have it in him, which was why he'd announced the day after the team's major league record sellout streak had ended on April 4, 2001, that he'd be leaving at the end of the season.

Shapiro took over in November and enacted his blueprint for success. Working with a smaller budget since the sellouts were no longer assured, he applied classic business principles to the remaking of the team. He and his staff compiled an extensive database on players and payroll, and Matt Tagliaferri developed a computer software program called Diamondview to track and analyze it. Predictably, the team slid to third place in the Central Division in 2002, and Joel Skinner replaced Manuel as manager in the middle of the season after a heated exchange between Shapiro and Manuel over Manuel's future with the team. For the 2003 season, Skinner was replaced by Eric Wedge, who'd been coaching prospects in the Indians minor leagues since 1998 and was named Minor League Manager of the Year in 2002 by *The Sporting News* after leading Triple A Buffalo to an 87–57 record. Presumably, in the major leagues Wedge would be coaching some of the players he'd helped develop in the minors. The Indians finished fourth in the Central Division in 2003 and third in 2004, but their farm system, under Director John Farrell, had improved to the point where it was named Organization of the Year in 2003 and 2004 by *USA Today Sports Weekly*. Those years

DID YOU KNOW . . . That Bob Wickman, fully recovered from Tommy John surgery on his right elbow in 2002, became the Indians' all-time saves leader when he picked up number 130 on May 7, 2006, when he protected a 2–0 lead at Seattle? Wickman, who tied for the American League lead with 45 saves in 2005, passed Doug Jones, who saved 129 games from 1986 to 1991 and 1998.

the Indians ranked third and fifth, respectively, in the major leagues in expenditures for scouting and player development.

Bolstered by that development, the Indians won 13 more games in 2005 than they did in 2004. Their 93–69 record left them in second place in the Central Division, but they went into the final weekend of the season with a chance to make the playoffs before being swept by the visiting Chicago White Sox, the eventual World Series champions they'd been trying to catch.

Shapiro was named Executive of the Year by *The Sporting News* and *Baseball America,* while Wedge received serious consideration for Manager of the Year.

No wonder expectations were high for 2006. With exciting young players like Sizemore and Travis Hafner, fans thought the team could overcome some radical changes on the pitching staff that dominated in 2005, when it led the American League with a 3.61 earned-run average.

But what's that they say about the best-laid plans? If the 2005 team overachieved, the 2006 team did the opposite. They lost early and they lost late. One day the pitching was horrible, the next day no one could hit. Their defense left a lot to be desired, too. At the All-Star break, they were mired in fourth place in the Central Division, 18½ games behind front-running Detroit. It was the furthest the team had been out since 1991—the year Hargrove was hired and the first rebuilding of the team began.

They finished the season with a 78–84 record. Nobody, from the front office on down, was satisfied with that result. It fueled their desire to make sure fans would have something to celebrate in 2007.

ANSWERS TO TRIVIA QUESTIONS

Page 5: Cap Anson and Honus Wagner were the first two players in baseball history to get 3,000 hits.

Page 9: To the surprise of sportswriters and fans alike, after the Indians won the 1920 Series Speaker made straight for the stands, where he gave his mother Jenny a long and heartfelt embrace.

Page 15: Jim Bagby holds the record for most wins by an Indians pitcher in a single season with 31 in 1920.

Page 18: The largest crowd ever in Cleveland Municipal Stadium was one of 125,000 that attended the National Eucharistic Congress in 1935.

Page 27: Pitcher Bob Feller was named to the All-Star team eight times, more than any other Indians player.

Page 29: The only two pitchers to play longer for one team than Mel Harder are Washington's Walter Johnson and the Chicago White Sox's Ted Lyons, who each played 21 seasons for his team.

Page 33: Jay Bell hit a home run in his first at-bat, on September 29, 1986, at Minnesota. Kevin Kouzmanoff hit a grand-slam home run on the first pitch he saw on September 2, 2006, at Texas.

Page 41: The name of the ballpark Bob Feller's father built on their Iowa farm was Oak View.

Page 44: Boudreau spent two days on the football team, trying out as a place-kicker.

Page 57: The other former major leaguer to join Doby in Japan in 1962 was Don Newcombe.

Page 67: Wes Ferrell holds the major league record for home runs by a pitcher with 38.

Page 71: Travis Hafner broke Rosen's record with six grand slams in 2006.

Page 83: White Sox shortstop Luis Aparicio beat out Colavito for the 1956 Rookie of the Year award.

Page 91: Ty Cobb's .366 is the all-time record for career batting average, and Rogers Hornsby is second at .358.

Page 99: Jim, two years older, was called "Goose," while Gaylord was called "Duck."

Page 108: General Manager Phil Seghi traded catcher Ken Suarez, outfielder Rusty Torres, and cash to the California Angels for Robinson on September 12, 1974.

Page 112: Mike Hargrove's real first name is Dudley.

Page 114: The Indians' Rookies of the Year are Herb Score in 1955, Chris Chambliss in 1971, Joe Charboneau in 1980, and Sandy Alomar Jr. in 1990.

Page 120: Ron Hassey—who caught Barker's perfect game and one by Dennis Martinez on July 28, 1991, when Montreal beat Los Angeles, 2–0, in Dodger Stadium—is the only catcher who caught two perfect games.

Page 126: After the 1993 season, the Indians granted Ojeda free agency, and he signed with the New York Yankees on January 28, 1994. He made two appearances with the Yankees. In three innings, he allowed 11 hits and eight runs. He was released by New York on May 5, 1994.

Page 133: Both are twins. Belle's twin is Terry; Thome's is Jennifer.

Page 141: Jim Thome's middle name is Howard.

Page 147: The highest-scoring game in World Series history was when Toronto beat Philadelphia 15–14 in four hours, 14 minutes in Game 4 of the 1993 World Series, which also made it the longest nine-inning game in World Series history.

Page 157: *Major League* was filmed in ballparks in Milwaukee and Baltimore.

Cleveland Indians All-Time Roster (through 2006 season)

Includes all players who have participated in one or more official American League games with Cleveland from 1901 through 2006. Players whose positions are indicated with a dash never played in the field and were used only as pinch runners, designated hitters, or pinch hitters.

A

Abbott, Fred (C, 1B)	1903–04
Abbott, Paul (P)	1993
Aber, Al (P)	1950–53
Abernathie, Bill (P)	1952
Abernathy, Ted (P)	1963–64
Ables, Harry (P)	1909
Adams, Bert (C)	1910–12
Adcock, Joe (1B)	1963
Agee, Tommie (OF)	1962–64
Aguayo, Luis (IF)	1989
Aguirre, Hank (P)	1955–57
Akerfelds, Darrel (P)	1987
Aldrete, Mike (1B, OF)	1991
Alexander, Bob (P)	1957
Alexander, Gary (C)	1978–80
Alexander, Hugh (OF)	1937
Allanson, Andy (C)	1986–89
Allen, Bob (P)	1961–63, 1966–67
Allen, Chad (OF)	2002
Allen, Johnny (P)	1936–40
Allen, Neil (P)	1989
Allen, Rod (—)	1988
Allison, Milo (OF)	1916–17
Allred, Beau (OF)	1989–91
Alomar, Roberto (2B)	1999–2001

Alomar, Sandy Jr. (C)	1990–2000
Alston, Dell (OF)	1979–80
Altizer, Dave (OF)	1908
Altobelli, Joe (1B)	1955, 57
Alvarado, Luis (2B)	1974
Alvis, Max (3B)	1962–69
Amaro, Ruben (OF)	1994–95
Andersen, Larry (P)	1975, 1977, 1979
Anderson, Brady (OF)	2002
Anderson, Brian (P)	1996–97, 2003
Anderson, Bud (P)	1982–83
Anderson, Dwain (2B)	1974
Anderson, Jason (P)	2004
Andrews, Ivy Paul (P)	1937
Andrews, Nate (P)	1940–41
Antonelli, John (P)	1961
Aponte, Luis (P)	1984
Arlin, Steve (P)	1974
Armstrong, Jack (P)	1992
Armstrong, Mike (P)	1987
Arnsberg, Brad (P)	1992
Ashby, Alan (C)	1973–76
Aspromonte, Ken (2B, 3B)	1960–62
Assenmacher, Paul (P)	1995–99
Atherton, Keith (P)	1989
Austin, Rick (P)	1970–71
Autry, Martin (C)	1926–28
Aven, Bruce (OF)	1997, 2002
Averill, Earl Jr. (C, 3B)	1956, 1958
Averill, Earl Sr. (OF)	1929–39
Avila, Bob (2B, 3B)	1949–58
Ayala, Benny (OF)	1985
Aylward, Dick (C)	1953
Azcue, Joe (C)	1963–69

B

Bacsik, Mike (P)	2001
Baerga, Carlos (IF)	1990–96, 1999
Baez, Danys (P)	2001–03
Bagby, James, Jr. (P)	1941–45
Bagby, James, Sr. (P)	1916–22
Bailes, Scott (P)	1986–89
Bailey, Steve (P)	1967–68
Baines, Harold (—)	1999
Baker, Bock (P)	1901
Baker, Brank (OF)	1969, 1971
Baker, Howard (3B)	1912
Ball, Neal (IF)	1909–12
Ballinger, Mark (P)	1971
Bando, Chris (C)	1981–88
Banks, George (OF, 3B)	1964–66
Bannister, Alan (OF, 2B)	1980–83
Barbare, Walter (3B)	1914–16
Barbeau, William (3B, 2B)	1905–06
Bard, Josh (C)	2002–05
Barker, Len (P)	1979–83
Barker, Ray (1B)	1965
Barkley, Jeff (P)	1984–85
Barnes, Brian (P)	1994
Barnes, Rich (P)	1983
Barnhart, Leslie (P)	1928, 1930
Bartosh, Cliff (P)	2004
Baskette, James (P)	1911–13
Bassler, Johnny (C)	1913–14
Bates, Ray (3B)	1913
Baxes, Jim (2B, 3B)	1959
Bay, Harry (OF)	1902–08
Bayne, William (P)	1928
Beall, John (OF)	1913
Bean, Belve (P)	1930–31, 1933–35
Bearden, Gene (P)	1947–50
Bearse, Kevin (P)	1990
Beck, Ervin (2B)	1901
Beck, George (P)	1914
Becker, Heinz (1B)	1946–47
Becker, Joe (C)	1936–37
Bedford, Gene (2B)	1925
Bedgood, Phil (P)	1922–23
Beebe, Fred (P)	1916
Beene, Fred (P)	1974–75
Behenna, Rick (P)	1983–85

Bell, Beau (OF, 1B)	1940–41
Bell, Buddy (3B, OF)	1972–78
Bell, David (2B)	1995, 1998
Bell, Eric (P)	1991–92
Bell, Gary (P)	1958–67
Bell, Jay (SS)	1986–88
Belle, Albert (OF)	1989–96
Belliard, Ronnie (2B)	2004–06
Bemis, Harry (C, 1B)	1902–10
Benge, Ray (P)	1925–26
Benjamin, Stan (OF)	1945
Benn, Henry (P)	1914
Benton, Al (P)	1949–50
Benton, Butch (C)	1985
Berardino, John (IF)	1948–50, 1952
Bere, Jason (P)	2000, 2003
Berg, Moe (C)	1931, 1934
Berger, Charles (P)	1907–10
Berger, Louis W. (2B, 1B)	1932, 1935–36
Bergman, Alfred H. (2B)	1916
Bernazard, Tony (2B)	1984–87
Bernhard, William (P)	1902–07
Berroa, Geronimo (OF)	1998
Berry, Joe (P)	1946
Berry, Ken (OF)	1975
Bescher, Robert (OF)	1918
Betancourt, Rafael (P)	2003–06
Bevacqua, Kurt (2B, OF)	1971–72
Beverlin, Jason (P)	2002
Bibby, Jim (P)	1975–77
Bielecki, Mike (P)	1993
Bierbrodt, Nick (P)	2003
Billings, Josh (C)	1913–18
Biras, Stephen (2B)	1944
Birmingham, Joe (OF, 3B)	1906–14
Bishop, Lloyd (P)	1914
Bisland, Rivington (SS)	1914
Black, Bud (P)	1988–90, 1995
Black, Don (P)	1946–48
Blaeholder, George (P)	1936
Blair, Willie (P)	1991
Blake, Casey (IF, OF)	2003–06
Blanco, Ossie (1B)	1974
Blanding, Fred (P)	1910–14
Blanks, Larvell (IF)	1976–78
Blyleven, Bert (P)	1981–85

Bochte, Bruce (OF, 3B)	1977
Bockman, Eddie (3B)	1947
Boehling, Joe (P)	1916–17, 1920
Bohnet, John (P)	1982
Boley, Joe (SS)	1932
Bolger, Jim (—)	1959
Bolton, Cecil (1B)	1928
Bond, Walter (OF)	1960–62
Bonds, Bobby (OF)	1979
Bonner, Frank (2B)	1902
Bonness, William (P)	1944
Booker, Richard (C)	1966
Booles, Seabron (P)	1909
Boone, Aaron (3B)	2005–06
Boone, Danny (P)	1922–23
Boone, Ray (SS)	1948–53
Borders, Pat (C)	1997–99
Bosman, Dick (P)	1973–75
Boss, Harley (1B)	1933
Boucher, Denis (P)	1991–92
Boudreau, Lou (SS, IF)	1938–50
Bowman, Abe (P)	1914–15
Bowsfield, Ted (P)	1960
Boyd, Gary (P)	1969
Boyd, Jason (P)	2003
Bracken, Jack (P)	1901
Bradford, Buddy (OF)	1970–71
Bradley, Bill (3B, SS)	1901–10
Bradley, John (C)	1916
Bradley, Milton (OF)	2001–03
Braggins, Richard (P)	1901
Branson, Jeff (2B, 3B)	1997–98
Branyan, Russell (OF, 3B)	1998–2002
Brennan, Addison (P)	1918
Brennan, Tom (P)	1981–83
Brenner, Delbert (P)	1912
Brenton, Lynn (P)	1913, 1915
Brenzel, Willam (C)	1934–35
Brewington, Jamie (P)	2000
Brewster, Charles (SS)	1946
Bridges, Rocky (SS, 3B)	1960
Briggs, Dan (OF)	1978
Briggs, John (P)	1959–60
Brissie, Lou (P)	1951–53
Broaca, John (P)	1939
Brodowski, Dick (P)	1958–59

Brohamer, Jack (2B)	1972–75, 1980
Brokens, Tom (3B, 2B)	1990
Bronkie, Herman (3B)	1910–12
Broussard, Ben (1B, OF)	2002–06
Brower, Frank (1B)	1923–24
Brower, Jim (P)	1999–2000
Brown, Andrew (P)	2006
Brown, Clint (P)	1928–35, 1941–42
Brown, Dick (C)	1957–59
Brown, Jackie (P)	1975–76
Brown, Larry (IF)	1963–71
Brown, Lloyd (P)	1934–37
Brown, Walter (P)	1927–28
Browne, Jerry (IF, OF)	1989–91
Buckeye, Garland (P)	1925–28
Buelow, Fred (C)	1904–06
Burba, Dave (P)	1998–2001, 2002
Burchart, Larry (P)	1969
Burks, Ellis (OF)	2001–03
Burnett, John (IF)	1927–34
Burnitz, Jeromy (OF)	1995–96
Burns, George (1B)	1920–21, 1924–28
Burton, Ellis (OF)	1963
Busby, Jim (OF)	1956–57
Buskey, Tom (P)	1974–77
Butcher, Henry (OF)	1911–12
Butcher, John (P)	1986
Butler, Bill (P)	1972
Butler, Brett (OF)	1984–87
Byrd, Paul (P)	2006

C

Cabrera, Fernando (P)	2004–06
Cabrera, Jolbert (OF, 2B)	1998–2002
Caffie, Joe (OF)	1956–57
Caffyn, Benjamin (OF)	1906
Cage, Wayne (1B)	1978–79
Cairncross, Cameron (P)	2000
Caldwell, Bruce (OF)	1928
Caldwell, Ray (P)	1919–21
Callahan, David (OF)	1910–11
Calvert, Paul (P)	1942–45
Camacho, Ernie (P)	1983–87
Camilli, Lou (IF)	1969–72
Campbell, Bruce (OF)	1935–39
Campbell, Clarence (OF)	1940–41

Camper, Cardell (P)	1977
Candaele, Casey (2B, 3B)	1996–97
Candiotti, Tom (P)	1986–91, 1999
Carbo, Bernie (—)	1978
Cardenal, Jose (OF)	1968–69
Cardenas, Leo (SS)	1973
Carisch, Fred (C)	1912–14
Carlton, Steve (P)	1987
Carmona, Fausto (P)	2006
Carnett, Ed (OF)	1945
Carr, Charles (1B)	1904–05
Carrasquel, Chico (SS, 3B)	1956–58
Carreon, Camilo (C)	1965
Carreon, Mark (1B, OF)	1996
Carson, Walter (OF)	1934–35
Carter, Joe (OF, 1B)	1984–89
Carter, Paul (P)	1914–15
Carty, Rico (1B, OF)	1974–77
Case, George (OF)	1946
Casey, Sean (1B)	1997
Casian, Larry (P)	1994
Castillo, Carmen (OF)	1982–88
Center, Earl (P)	1942–43, 1945–46
Cermak, Edward (OF)	1901
Cerone, Rick (C)	1975–76
Chakales, Bob (P)	1951–54
Chambliss, Chris (1B)	1971–74
Chance, Bob (1B, OF)	1963–64
Chance, Dean (P)	1970
Chapman, Ben (OF)	1939–40
Chapman, Ray (SS, IF)	1912–20
Chapman, Sam (OF)	1951
Chappell, Larry (—)	1916
Charboneau, Joe (OF)	1980–82
Chech, Charles (P)	1908
Cheeves, Virgil (P)	1924
Choo, Shin-Soo (OF)	2006
Christopher, Mike (P)	1992–93
Christopher, Russ (P)	1948
Churn, Clarence (P)	1958
Cicotte, Al (P)	1959
Cihocki, Al (IF)	1945
Cissell, Chalmer (2B, SS)	1932–33
Clanton, Ucal (1B)	1922
Clark, Allie (OF)	1948–51
Clark, Bryan (P)	1985

Clark, Dave (OF)	1986–89
Clark, Harvey (P)	1902
Clark, James (OF)	1971
Clark, Mark (P)	1993–95
Clark, Robert (P)	1920–21
Clark, Terry (P)	1997
Clark, William (P)	1924
Clarke, Joshua (OF)	1908–09
Clarke, Justin (C)	1905–10
Clarke, Sumpter (OF)	1923–24
Clarkson, Walter (P)	1907–08
Cline, Ty (OF)	1960–62
Clingman, William (2B)	1903
Clinton, Lou (OF)	1965
Clyde, David (P)	1978–79
Codiroli, Chris (P)	1988
Colavito, Rocky (OF)	1955–59, 1965–67
Colbert, Vince (P)	1970–72
Cole, Albert (P)	1925
Cole, Alex (OF)	1990–92
Coleman, Gordon (1B)	1959
Coleman, Robert (C)	1916
Collamore, Al (P)	1914–15
Collard, Earl (P)	1927–28
Collins, Don (P)	1980
Collum, Jackie (P)	1962
Colon, Bartolo (P)	1997–2002
Combs, Merrill (SS)	1951–52
Comer, Steve (P)	1984
Congalton, William (OF)	1905–07
Connally, George (P)	1931–34
Connatser, Bruce (1B)	1931–32
Connolly, Ed (P)	1967
Connolly, Joe (OF)	1922–23
Connor, Joseph (C)	1901
Constable, Jim (P)	1958
Conway, Jack (2B, SS)	1941, 1946–47
Conyers, Herb (1B)	1950
Cook, Dennis (P)	1992–93, 1995
Cora, Alex (SS)	2005
Cora, Joey (2B)	1998
Cordero, Wil (OF)	1999, 2000–02
Cordova, Marty (OF)	2001
Cortes, David (P)	2003
Coughtry, Marlan (—)	1962
Coumbe, Fred (P)	1914–19

Coveleski, Stan (P)	1916–24
Cox, Ted (3B, OF)	1978–79
Craghead, Howard (P)	1931–33
Craig, Rodney (OF)	1982
Crandall, Del (C)	1966
Creel, Keith (P)	1985
Cressend, Jack (P)	2003–04
Crisp, Coco (OF)	2002–05
Cristall, William (P)	1901
Crosby, Ed (IF)	1974–76
Cross, Frank (OF)	1901
Cruceta, Francisco (P)	2004
Cruz, Jacob (OF)	1998–2001
Cruz, Victor (P)	1979–80
Cullenbine, Roy (OF, 1B)	1943–45
Cullop, Henry (OF)	1927
Cullop, Nick (P)	1913–14
Culmer, Wil (OF)	1983
Culver, George (P)	1966–67
Curry, Tony (—)	1966
Curtis, Chad (OF)	1997
Curtis, Jack (P)	1963
Cypert, Al (3B)	1914

D

Dade, Paul (OF, 3B)	1977–79
Dailey, Bill (P)	1961–62
Dalena, Pete (—)	1989
Daley, Bud (P)	1955–57
Daly, Tom (C)	1916
D'Amico, Jeff (P)	2004
Dashner, Lee (P)	1913
Davalillo, Vic (OF)	1963–68
Davidson, Homer (C)	1908
Davis, Bill (1B)	1965–66
Davis, Harry (1B)	1912
Davis, Jason (P)	2002–06
Davis, Kane (P)	2000
Davis, Steve (P)	1989
Dawley, Joe (P)	2004
Dawson, Joe (P)	1924
Dean, Alfred (P)	1941–43
DeBerry, Hank (C)	1916–17
Dedmon, Jeff (P)	1988
Delahanty, Frank (OF)	1907
de la Hoz, Mike (IF)	1960–63

DeLucia, Rich (P)	1999
Demeter, Don (OF)	1967
Demeter, Steve (3B)	1960
DeMott, Ben (P)	1910–11
Dempsey, Rick (C)	1987
Denney, Kyle (P)	2004
Denning, Otto (C, 1B)	1942–43
Denny, John (P)	1980–82
Dente, Sam (IF)	1954–55
DePaula, Sean (P)	1999–2000, 2002
Desautels, Gene (C)	1941–43, 1945
Des Jardien, Paul (P)	1916
Detore, George (3B, SS)	1930–31
Devlin, James (C)	1944
Diaz, Bo (C)	1978–81
Diaz, Einar (C)	1996–2002
Dicken, Paul (—)	1964, 1966
Dickerson, George (P)	1917
Dillard, Don (OF)	1959–62
Dillinger, Harley (P)	1914
Dilone, Miguel (OF)	1980–83
DiPoto, Jerry (P)	1993–94
Doane, Walter (P)	1909–10
Dobson, Joe (P)	1939–40
Dobson, Pat (P)	1976–77
Doby, Larry (OF)	1947–55, 1958
Doljack, Frank (OF)	1943
Donahue, Francis (P)	1903–05
Donahue, Patrick (C)	1910
Donohue, Peter (P)	1931
Donovan, Dick (P)	1962–65
Donovan, Mike (SS)	1904
Donovan, Thomas (OF)	1901
Doran, William (3B)	1922
Dorman, Dwight (OF)	1928
Dorner, August (P)	1902–03
Dorsett, Brian (C)	1987
Dorsett, Calvin (P)	1940–41, 1947
Dowling, Peter (P)	1901
Drake, Logan (P)	1922–24
Drake, Thomas (P)	1939
Drese, Ryan (P)	2001–02
Drew, Tim (P)	2000–01
Dubois, Jason (OF)	2005
Duffy, Frank (SS)	1972–77
Duncan, Dave (C)	1973–74

Dunlop, George (SS)	1913–14	Evers, Hoot (OF)	1955–56
Dunning, Steve (P)	1970–73		
Dunston, Shawon (2B, SS, OF)	1998	**F**	
Dunwoody, Todd (OF)	2002	Faeth, Tony (P)	1919–20
Durbin, Chad (P)	2003–04	Fahr, Gerald (P)	1951
Dybzinski, Jerry (IF)	1980–82	Fain, Ferris (1B)	1955
Dyck, James (—)	1954	Falk, Bibb (OF)	1929–31
		Falkenberg, Fred (P)	1908–11, 1913
E		Fanwell, Harry (P)	1910
Eagan, Charles (2B)	1901	Farmer, Ed (P)	1971–73
Easter, Luke (1B, OF)	1949–54	Farmer, Jack (3B)	1918
Easterly, Jamie (P)	1983–87	Farr, Steve (P)	1984, 1994
Easterly, Ted (C, OF)	1909–12	Farrell, John (P)	1987–90, 1995
Eckersley, Dennis (P)	1975–77	Feller, Bob (P)	1936–41, 1945–56
Edmondson, George (P)	1922–24	Fermin, Felix (SS)	1989–93
Edmonson, Ed (OF, 1B)	1913	Fernandez, Tony (2B)	1997
Edwards, Doc (C)	1962–63	Ferrarese, Don (P)	1958–59
Edwards, Hank (OF)	1941–43, 1946–49	Ferrell, Wesley (P)	1927–33
Edwards, Jim (P)	1922–25	Ferrick, Tom (P)	1942, 1946
Eells, Harry (P)	1906	Ferry, Alfred (P)	1905
Egan, Arthur (C)	1914–15	Fewster, Chick (2B)	1924–25
Eglof, Bruce (P)	1991	Fielder, Cecil (1B)	1998
Eibel, Henry (OF)	1912	Finley, Chuck (P)	2000–02
Eichelberger, Juan (P)	1983	Firova, Dan (C)	1988
Eichrodt, Fred (OF)	1925–27	Fischer, Carl (P)	1937
Eisenstat, Harry (P)	1939–42	Fischlin, Mike (2B, 3B, SS)	1981–85
Elarton, Scott (P)	2004–05	Fisher, Ed (P)	1968
Elder, Dave (P)	2002–03	Fisher, Gus (C)	1911
Ellerbe, Frank (3B)	1924	Fitz Gerald, Ed (C)	1959
Ellingsen, Bruce (P)	1974	Fitzke, Paul (P)	1924
Ellis, John (C, 1B)	1973–75	Fitzmorris, Al (P)	1977–78
Ellison, George (P)	1920	Flanigan, Ray (P)	1946
Ellsworth, Dick (P)	1969–70	Fleming, Les (1B, OF)	1941–42, 1945–47
Embree, Alan (P)	1992, 1995–96	Flick, Elmer (OF)	1902–10
Embree, Charles (P)	1941–42, 1944–47	Flores, Jesse (P)	1950
Engel, Joe (P)	1919	Foiles, Hank (C)	1953, 1955–56, 1960
Engle, Arthur (3B)	1916	Fonseca, Lew (1B, 2B)	1927–31
Enzmann, John (P)	1918–19	Ford, Ted (OF)	1970–71, 1973
Eschen, James (OF)	1915	Fosse, Ray (C, 1B)	1967–72, 1976–77
Escobar, Alex (OF)	2003–04	Foster, Alan (P)	1971
Escobar, Jose (SS)	1991	Foster, Edward (P)	1908
Espinoza, Alvaro (IF)	1993–96	Foster, Roy (OF)	1970–72
Essegian, Chuck (OF)	1961–62	Franco, Julio (SS, 2B)	1983–88, 1996–97
Essian, Jim (C)	1983	Francona, Terry (—)	1988
Eunick, Fernandas (3B)	1917	Francona, Tito (OF, 1B)	1959–64
Evans, Joe (3B, OF, SS)	1915–22	Frazier, George (P)	1984

Frazier, Joe (OF)	1947
Freiburger, Vernon (1B)	1941
Freisleben, Dave (P)	1978
Fridley, Jim (OF)	1952
Friend, Owen (2B)	1953
Frierson, Robert (OF)	1941
Frobel, Doug (OF)	1987
Fry, Johnson (P)	1923
Fryman, Travis (3B)	1998–2002
Fuller, Vern (2B, 3B)	1964, 1966–70
Funk, Frank (P)	1960–62

G

Gaffke, Fabian (OF)	1941–42
Gagliano, Ralph (—)	1965
Galatzer, Milton (OF)	1933–36
Galehouse, Dennis (P)	1934–38
Gallagher, Charlie (OF)	1901
Gallagher, Dave (OF)	1987
Gallagher, Jackie (OF)	1923
Gamble, Oscar (OF)	1973–75
Gandil, Charles (1B)	1916
Garbark, Robert (C)	1934–35
Garcia, Karim (OF)	2001–03
Garcia, Mike (P)	1948–59
Gardner, Larry (3B)	1919–24
Gardner, Ray (SS)	1929–30
Gardner, Rob (P)	1968
Garko, Ryan (1B)	2005–06
Garland, Wayne (P)	1977–81
Garrett, Clarence (P)	1915
Gassaway, Charles (P)	1946
Geiger, Gary (OF)	1958
Genins, Frank (OF)	1901
Gentile, Jim (—)	1966
George, Charles (C)	1935–36
George, Lefty (P)	1912
Gerken, George (OF)	1927–28
Gerut, Jody (OF)	2003–05
Gettel, Al (P)	1947–48
Getz, Gus (3B)	1918
Gil, Gus (2B)	1967
Giles, Brian (OF)	1995–98
Gill, John (OF)	1927–28
Ginn, Tinsley (OF)	1914
Ginsberg, Joe (C)	1953–54

Glavenich, Luke (P)	1913
Gleeson, James (OF)	1936
Glendon, Martin (P)	1903
Gliatto, Salvador (P)	1930
Glynn, Bill (1B)	1952–54
Glynn, Ed (P)	1981–83
Gochnaur, John (SS)	1902–03
Gogolewski, Bill (P)	1974
Goldman, Jonah (SS, 3B)	1928, 1930–31
Gomez, Ruben (P)	1962
Gonzales, Rene (3B)	1994
Gonzalez, Denny (—)	1989
Gonzalez, Jose (OF)	1991
Gonzalez, Juan (OF)	2001, 2005
Gonzalez, Orlando (1B)	1976
Gonzalez, Pedro (2B)	1965–67
Gonzalez, Raul (OF)	2004
Gooch, Lee (—)	1915
Good, Wilbur (OF)	1908–09
Gooden, Dwight (P)	1998–99
Gordon, Don (P)	1987–88
Gordon, Joe (2B)	1947–50
Gould, Al (P)	1916–17
Gozzo, Mauro (P)	1990–91
Graber, Rod (OF)	1958
Graham, George (2B)	1902
Gramly, Tom (P)	1968
Graney, Jack (OF)	1908, 1910–22
Grant, Edward (2B)	1905
Grant, George (P)	1927–29
Grant, James (2B)	1943–44
Grant, Jim (P)	1958–64
Grasso, Mickey (C)	1954
Graves, Danny (P)	1996, 2006
Gray, Gary (—)	1980
Gray, John (P)	1957
Gray, Ted (P)	1955
Green, Gene (OF)	1962–63
Gregg, David (P)	1913
Gregg, Vean (P)	1911–14
Griffin, Alfredo (SS)	1976–78
Griggs, Arthur (1B, 2B)	1911–12
Grim, Bob (P)	1960
Grimes, Oscar (IF)	1938–42
Grimsley, Jason (P)	1993–95
Grimsley, Ross (P)	1980

Grissom, Marquis (OF)	1997	Harris, Mickey (P)	1952
Gromek, Steve (P)	1941–53	Harrison, Roric (P)	1975
Groom, Robert (P)	1918	Harshman, Jack (P)	1959–60
Groth, Ernie (P)	1947–48	Harstad, Oscar (P)	1915
Grubb, Harvey (3B)	1912	Hart, William (P)	1901
Grubb, Johnny (OF)	1977–78	Hartford, Bruce (SS)	1914
Guante, Cecilio (P)	1990	Hartley, Grover (C)	1929–30
Guisto, Louis (1B)	1916–17, 1921–23	Hartman, Bob (P)	1962
Gulley, Thomas (OF)	1923–24	Harvel, Luther (OF)	1928
Gunkel, Woodward (P)	1916	Harvey, Erwin (OF)	1901–02
Guthrie, Jeremy (P)	2004–06	Hassey, Ron (C, 1B)	1978–84
Gutierrez, Franklin (OF)	2005–06	Hatfield, Fred (3B)	1958
Gutierrez, Ricky (2B)	2002–03	Hauger, John (OF)	1912
		Hauser, Joe (1B)	1929
H		Havens, Brad (P)	1988–89
Hafner, Travis (1B)	2003–06	Hawkins, Wynn (P)	1960–62
Hagerman, Zeriah (P)	1914–16	Haworth, Howard (C)	1915
Hale, Bob (1B)	1960–61	Hayes, Frank (C)	1945–46
Hale, Odell (2B, 3B)	1931, 1933–40	Hayes, Von (OF, 3B)	1981–82
Hall, Jimmie (OF)	1968–69	Heath, Jeff (OF)	1936–45
Hall, Mel (OF)	1984–88	Heaton, Neal (P)	1982–86
Hall, Russell (SS)	1901	Hedlund, Mike (P)	1965, 1968
Halla, John (P)	1905	Heffner, Bob (P)	1966
Hallman, Bill (SS)	1901	Hegan, Jim (C)	1941–42, 1946–57
Halt, Alva (3B)	1918	Heidemann, Jack (SS)	1969–72, 1974
Hamann, Elmer (P)	1922	Held, Woodie (IF, OF)	1958–64
Hamilton, Jack (P)	1969	Helf, Henry (C)	1938, 1940
Hamilton, Steve (P)	1961	Heman, Russ (P)	1961
Hammond, Walter (2B)	1915, 1922	Hemphill, Charles (OF)	1902
Hamner, Granny (SS)	1959	Hemsley, Rollie (C)	1938–41
Hand, Rich (P)	1970–71	Henderson, Bernard (P)	1921
Haney, Chris (P)	1999–2000	Hendrick, George (OF)	1973–76
Hansen, Doug (—)	1951	Hendrick, Harvey (1B)	1925
Harder, Mel (P)	1928–47	Hendryx, Tim (OF)	1911–12
Hardy, Carroll (OF)	1958–60	Hengel, Dave (OF)	1989
Hardy, John (OF)	1903	Hennigan, Phil (P)	1969–72
Hargan, Steve (P)	1965–72	Henry, Earl (P)	1944–45
Hargrove, Mike (1B, OF)	1979–85	Hermoso, Angel (2B)	1974
Harkness, Fred (P)	1910–11	Hernandez, Jeremy (P)	1993
Harper, Tommy (OF)	1968	Hernandez, Jose (SS)	1992, 2005
Harrah, Toby (3B, SS)	1979–83	Hernandez, Keith (1B)	1990
Harrell, Billy (SS, 3B)	1955, 1957–58	Herrera, Alex (P)	2002–03
Harrelson, Ken (OF, 1B)	1969–71	Hershiser, Orel (P)	1995–97
Harris, Billy (2B, 3B)	1968	Hess, Otto (P, OF)	1902, 1904–08
Harris, Charles (P)	1951	Heving, Joe (P)	1937–38, 1941–44
Harris, Joe (1B)	1917, 1919	Hickey, John (P)	1904

Hickman, Charles (1B, 2B, OF)	1902–04, 1909	Hughes, Roy (IF)	1935–37
Higgins, Bob (C)	1909	Huismann, Mark (P)	1987
Higgins, Dennis (P)	1970	Humphries, John (P)	1938–40
Higgins, Mark (1B)	1989	Hunnefield, William (SS)	1931
Hillegas, Shawn (P)	1991	Hunter, Billy (SS)	1958
Hildebrand, Oral (P)	1931–36	Hunter, William (OF)	1912
Hilgendorf, Tom (P)	1972–74		
Hill, Glenallen (OF)	1991–93	**I**	
Hill, Herb (P)	1915	Inglett, Joe (IF)	2006
Hill, Hugh (—)	1903	Iott, Fred (OF)	1903
Hill, Ken (P)	1995	Irwin, Thomas (SS)	1938
Hinchman, Harry (2B)	1907		
Hinchman, William (OF, SS)	1907–09	**J**	
Hinton, Chuck (OF, IF)	1965–67, 1969–71	Jablonowski, Pete (P)	1930–32*
Hinzo, Tommy (2B)	1987, 1989	Jackson, Damian (SS, 2B)	1996–97
Hoag, Myril (OF)	1944–45	Jackson, Jimmy (OF)	1905–06
Hockett, Oris (OF)	1941–44	Jackson, Joe (OF)	1910–15
Hodapp, John (IF)	1925–32	Jackson, Michael R. (P)	1997–99
Hodge, Harold (IF)	1971	Jackson, Michael W. (P)	1973
Hoffer, Bill (P)	1901	Jackson, Randy (3B)	1958–59
Hoffman, Edward (3B)	1915	Jacobson, Bill (OF)	1927
Hogan, Harry (OF)	1901	Jacoby, Brook (3B, 1B)	1984–92
Hogan, Ken (—)	1923–24	Jacome, Jason (P)	1997–98
Hohnhorst, Ed (1B)	1910, 1912	James, Chris (OF, 1B)	1990–91
Holland, Robert (OF)	1934	James, Dion (OF, 1B)	1989–90
Hollandsworth, Todd (OF)	2006	James, Lefty (P)	1912–14
Hollins, Dave (—)	2001	James, William H. (P)	1911–12
Holloway, Ken (P)	1929–30	Jamieson, Charles (OF)	1919–32
Hood, Don (P)	1975–79	Jasper, Harry (P)	1919
Hooper, Bob (P)	1953–54	Jeanes, Ernest (OF)	1921–22
Horn, Sam (—)	1993	Jeffcoat, Mike (P)	1983–85
Horton, Tony (1B)	1967–70	Jefferson, Reggie (1B)	1991–93
Horton, Willie (—)	1978	Jefferson, Stan (OF)	1990
Hoskins, Dave (P)	1953–54	Jessee, Dan (—)	1929
Houston, Tyler (3B, C)	1999	Jeter, John (OF)	1974
Houtteman, Art (P)	1953–57	Jimenez, Houston (2B)	1988
Howard, Doug (1B)	1976	Jimenez, Jose (P)	2004
Howard, Ivan (2B)	1916–17	John, Tommy (P)	1963–64
Howard, Thomas (OF)	1992–93	Johnson, Alex (OF)	1972
Howell, Millard (P)	1940	Johnson, Bob (P)	1974
Howell, Murray (—)	1941	Johnson, Cliff (—)	1979–80
Howry, Bob (P)	2004–05	Johnson, Jerry (P)	1973
Howser, Dick (SS, 2B)	1963–66	Johnson, Larry D. (C)	1972, 1974
Hubbard, Trenidad (OF)	1997		
Hudlin, Willis (P)	1926–40	* Pete Jablonowski legally changed his name to Pete	
Huff, Mike (OF)	1991	Appleton in 1933.	

Johnson, Lou (OF)	1968	Kindall, Jerry (2B, SS)	1962–64
Johnson, Victor (P)	1946	Kiner, Ralph (OF)	1955
Johnston, Doc (1B)	1912–14, 1918–21	King, Eric (P)	1991
Jones, Doug (P)	1986–91, 1998	King, Jim (OF)	1967
Jones, Hal (1B)	1961–62	Kinney, Dennis (P)	1978
Jones, Sam P. (P)	1914–15	Kirby, Wayne (OF)	1991–96
Jones, Sam (P)	1951–52	Kirke, Jay (1B, OF)	1914–15
Jones, Willie (3B)	1959	Kirkland, Willie (OF)	1961–63
Jordan, Scott (OF)	1988	Kirsch, Harry (P)	1910
Jordan, Tom (C)	1946	Kiser, Garland (P)	1991
Joss, Adrian (P)	1902–10	Kittle, Ron (—)	1988
Juden, Jeff (P)	1997	Kittridge, Malachi (C)	1906
Judnich, Walt (OF, 1B)	1948	Klein, Louis (—)	1951
Jungels, Ken (P)	1937–38, 1940–41	Kleine, Harold (P)	1944–45
Justice, David (OF)	1997–2000	Klepfer, Ed (P)	1915–17, 1919
		Klieman, Ed (P)	1943–48
K		Klimchock, Lou (3B, 2B)	1968–70
Kahdot, Isaac (3B)	1922	Kline, Steven Jack (P)	1974
Kahl, Nick (2B)	1905	Kline, Steven James (P)	1997
Kahler, George (P)	1910–14	Klippstein, John (P)	1960
Kaiser, Bob (P)	1971	Klugmann, Joe (2B)	1925
Kaiser, Jeff (P)	1987–90	Knaupp, Henry (SS)	1910–11
Kamieniecki, Scott (P)	2000	Knickerbocker, William (SS)	1933–36
Kamm, William (3B)	1931–35	Knode, Robert (1B)	1923–26
Kardow, Paul (P)	1936	Koestner, Elmer (P)	1910
Karr, Ben (P)	1925–27	Komminsk, Brad (OF)	1989
Karsay, Steve (P)	1998–2001	Kopf, William (2B)	1913
Kavanagh, Martin (1B)	1916–18	Kouzmanoff, Kevin (—)	2006
Keedy, Pat (OF)	1989	Krakauskas, Joe (P)	1941–42, 1946
Keefe, David (P)	1922	Kralick, Jack (P)	1963–67
Kekich, Mike (P)	1973	Kramer, Tom (P)	1991, 1993
Kelley, Tom (P)	1964–67	Krapp, Gene (P)	1911–12
Kelly, Bob (P)	1958	Krause, Harry (P)	1912
Kelly, Pat (—)	1981	Kreuger, Rick (P)	1978
Keltner, Ken (3B)	1937–44, 1946–49	Krivda, Rick (P)	1998
Kendall, Fred (C)	1977	Kroll, Gary (P)	1969
Kennedy, Bill (P)	1948	Kroner, John (2B, 3B)	1937–38
Kennedy, Bob (OF, 3B)	1948–54	Krueger, Ernest (C)	1913
Kennedy, Vernon (P)	1942–44	Kruger, Arthur (OF)	1910
Kenney, Jerry (2B)	1973	Kubiszyn, Jack (SS)	1961–62
Kent, Jeff (IF)	1996	Kuenn, Harvey (OF)	1960
Keough, Marty (OF)	1960	Kuhn, Bernard (P)	1924
Kern, Jim (P)	1974–78, 1986	Kuhn, Kenny (SS, 2B)	1955–57
Kibble, John (3B)	1912	Kuiper, Duane (2B)	1974–81
Kilkenny, Mike (P)	1972–73	Kurtz, Hal (P)	1968
Killian, Ed (P)	1903	Kuzava, Bob (P)	1946–47

L

Lacey, Bob (P)	1981
LaChance, George (1B)	1901
Lacy, Osceola (2B)	1926
Lajoie, Napoleon (IF)	1902–14
Laker, Tim (C)	2001–04, 2006
Lamb, Ray (P)	1971–73
Lambeth, Otis (P)	1916–18
Lampkin, Tom (C)	1988
Land, Grover (C)	1908–11, 1913
Landis, Jim (OF)	1966
Langford, Elton (OF)	1927–28
Langston, Mark (P)	1999
Lara, Juan (P)	2006
LaRocca, Greg (3B)	2002–03
LaRoche, Dave (P)	1975–77
Lary, Lyn (SS)	1937–39
Lasher, Fred (P)	1970
Laskey, Bill (P)	1988
Latman, Barry (P)	1960–63
Lattimore, William (P)	1908
Law, Ron (P)	1969
Lawrence, Jim (C)	1963
Lawson, Roxie (P)	1930–31
Lawton, Matt (OF)	2002–04
Laxton, Bill (P)	1977
Leber, Emil (3B)	1905
Ledee, Ricky (OF)	2000
Lee, Clifford (OF)	1925–26
Lee, Clifton (P)	2002–06
Lee, Dave (P)	2003–04
Lee, Leron (OF)	1974–75
Lee, Mike (P)	1960
Lee, Thornton (P)	1933–36
Leek, Gene (3B)	1959
Lehner, Paul (OF)	1951
Lehr, Norman (P)	1926
Leibold, Harry (OF)	1913–15
Leitner, George (P)	1902
Leius, Scott (3B, 2B)	1996
Lelivelt, Jack (OF)	1913–14
LeMaster, Johnnie (SS)	1985
Lemon, Bob (P, OF)	1941–42, 1946–58
Lemon, Jim (OF)	1950, 1953
Leon, Eddie (2B, SS)	1968–72

Leonard, Joseph (2B)	1916
Levis, Jesse (C)	1992–95, 1999
Levsen, Dutch (P)	1923–28
Lewallyn, Dennis (P)	1981–82
Lewis, Mark (SS, 2B)	1991–94, 2001
Liebhardt, Glenn (P)	1906–09
Liefer, Jeff (1B, OF)	2005
Lilliquist, Derek (P)	1992–94
Lind, Carl (2B)	1927–30
Linde, Lyman (P)	1947–48
Lindsay, William (3B)	1911
Lindsey, Jim (P)	1922, 1924
Link, Fred (P)	1910
Lintz, Larry (—)	1978
Lipski, Bob (C)	1963
Lis, Joe (1B)	1974–76
Lister, Peter (1B)	1907
Little, Mark (OF)	2004
Littleton, Larry (OF)	1981
Livingston, Paddy (C)	1901, 1912
Locke, Bobby (P)	1959–61
Locklin, Stu (OF)	1955–56
Lofton, Kenny (OF)	1992–96, 1998–2001
Lohr, Howard (OF)	1916
Lolich, Ron (OF)	1972–73
Lollar, Sherm (C)	1946
Lopez, Al (C)	1947
Lopez, Albie (P)	1993–97
Lopez, Luis (C, 1B)	1991
Lopez, Marcelino (P)	1972
Lord, Bristol (OF)	1909–10
Lorraine, Andrew (P)	2000
Lovullo, Torey (2B, 3B)	1998
Lowdermilk, Grover (P)	1916
Lowenstein, John (OF, IF)	1970–77
Ludwick, Ryan (OF)	2003–05
Luke, Matt (—)	1998
Luna, Hector (2B)	2006
Lund, Gordon (SS)	1967
Lundbom, John (P)	1902
Lunte, Harry (SS)	1919–20
Luplow, Al (OF)	1961–65
Lush, William (OF)	1904
Lutzke, Walter (3B, 2B)	1923–27
Lyon, Russell (C)	1944

M

Machemehl, Charles (P)	1971
Mack, Ray (2B)	1938–44, 1946
Mackiewicz, Felix (OF)	1945–47
Maddern, Clarence (OF)	1951
Magallanes, Ever (SS)	1991
Maglie, Sal (P)	1955–56
Magrann, Tom (C)	1989
Magruder, Chris (OF)	2002–03
Mahoney, Jim (SS)	1962
Mails, John (P)	1920–22
Majeski, Henry (2B, 3B)	1952–55
Maldonado, Candy (OF)	1990, 1993–94
Manning, Rick (OF)	1975–83
Manto, Jeff (3B, 1B)	1990–91, 1997–99
Maris, Roger (OF)	1957–58
Marsh, Fred (—)	1949
Marte, Andy (IF)	2006
Martin, Billy (2B)	1959
Martin, Morris (P)	1958
Martin, Tom (P)	1998–2000
Martinez, Carlos (1B, 3B)	1991–93
Martinez, Dennis (P)	1994–96
Martinez, Sandy (C)	2004
Martinez, Tony (SS)	1963–66
Martinez, Victor (C, 1B)	2002–06
Martinez, Willie (P)	2000
Mastny, Tom (P)	2006
Mathias, Carl (P)	1960
Maurer, Dave (P)	2002
Maye, Lee (OF)	1967–69
McAleer, James (OF)	1901
McBride, Bake (OF)	1982–83
McCabe, Ralph (P)	1946
McCarthy, Jack (OF)	1901–03
McCosky, Barney (OF)	1951–53
McCraw, Tom (1B, OF)	1972, 1974–75
McCrea, Francis (C)	1925
McDonald, John (2B, SS)	1999–2004
McDonnell, Jim (C)	1943–45
McDowell, Jack (P)	1996–97
McDowell, Oddibe (OF)	1989
McDowell, Sam (P)	1961–71
McGuire, James A. (SS)	1901
McGuire, James T. (C)	1908, 1910
McHale, Martin (P)	1916

McInnis, John (1B)	1922
McKain, Harold (P)	1927
McLemore, Mark (3B)	1990
McLish, Cal (P)	1956–59
McMahon, Don (P)	1964–66
McNeal, John (P)	1901
McNulty, Pat (OF)	1922, 1924–27
McQuilan, George (P)	1918
Medina, Luis (1B)	1988–89, 1991
Meixell, Merten (OF)	1912
Mele, Sam (OF)	1956
Melton, Bill (1B, 3B)	1977
Mercker, Kent (P)	1996
Merloni, Lou (IF)	2004–06
Merullo, Matt (C)	1994
Mesa, Jose (P)	1992–98
Messenger, Andrew (P)	1924
Metivier, George (P)	1922–24
Metkovich, George (OF)	1947
Meyer, Lambert (2B)	1945–46
Miceli, Dan (P)	2003
Michaels, Jason (OF)	2006
Middleton, John (P)	1922
Milacki, Bob (P)	1993
Milbourne, Larry (2B, SS)	1982
Miljus, John (P)	1928–29
Miller, Edwin (1B)	1918
Miller, Matt (P)	2004–06
Miller, Raymond (1B)	1917
Miller, Robert (P)	1970
Miller, Walter (P)	1924–31
Milligan, Randy (1B)	1993
Mills, Abbott (3B)	1911
Mills, Buster (OF)	1942, 1946
Mills, Frank (C)	1914
Millwood, Kevin (P)	2005
Milnar, Al (P)	1936, 1938–43
Mingori, Steve (P)	1970–73
Minoso, Minnie (OF)	1949, 1951, 1958–59
Mitchell, Dale (OF)	1946–56
Mitchell, Kevin (OF)	1997
Mitchell, Willie (P)	1909–16
Mlicki, Dave (P)	1992–93
Moeller, Dan (OF)	1916
Mohler, Mike (P)	2000
Monaco, Blas (2B)	1937, 1946

Monge, Sid (P)	1977–81
Montague, Edward (SS, 3B)	1928, 1930–32
Moon, Leo (P)	1932
Moore, Barry (P)	1970
Moore, Earl (P)	1901–07
Moore, Edward (2B)	1934
Moore, James (P)	1928–29
Mora, Andres (OF)	1980
Moran, Billy (IF)	1958–59, 1964–65
Morgan, Eddie (1B, OF, 3B)	1928–33
Morgan, Joe (3B)	1960–61
Morman, Alvin (P)	1997–98
Moronko, Jeff (3B)	1984
Morris, Jack (P)	1994
Morton, Guy (P)	1914–24
Moses, Gerry (C)	1972
Moss, Howard (3B)	1946
Mossi, Don (P)	1954–58
Mota, Guillermo (P)	2006
Mujica, Edward (P)	2006
Mulholland, Terry (P)	2002–03
Mullins, Fran (2B, SS)	1986
Muncrief, Bob (P)	1948
Murchison, Thomas (P)	1920
Murray, Eddie (1B)	1994–96
Murray, Heath (P)	2002
Murray, Ray (C)	1948, 1950–51
Mutis, Jeff (P)	1991–93
Myatt, Glenn (C)	1923–35
Myers, Elmer (P)	1919–20
Myette, Aaron (P)	2003

N

Nabholz, Chris (P)	1994
Nagelsen, Louis (C)	1912
Nagelson, Russ (OF)	1968–70
Nagy, Charles (P)	1990–2002
Nahorodny, Bill (C)	1982
Naragon, Hal (C)	1951, 1954–59
Narleski, Ray (P)	1954–58
Nash, Ken (SS)	1912
Navarro, Jamie (P)	2000
Naymick, Mike (P)	1939–40, 1943–44
Neeman, Cal (C)	1963
Neher, James (P)	1912
Neis, Bernie (OF)	1927

Nelson, Dave (2B, SS)	1968–69
Nelson, Rocky (1B)	1954
Nettles, Graig (3B)	1970–72
Netzel, Milo (3B)	1909
Newcombe, Don (P)	1960
Newhouser, Hal (P)	1954–55
Newman, Al (P)	2000
Nicholls, Simon (SS)	1910
Nichols, Rod (P)	1988–92
Nichting, Chris (P)	2000
Niehaus, Richard (P)	1920
Niekro, Phil (P)	1986–87
Nielsen, Milt (OF)	1949, 1951
Nieman, Bob (OF)	1961–62
Niles, Harry (OF)	1910
Nill, George (SS)	1907–08
Nipper, Al (P)	1990
Nischwitz, Ron (P)	1963
Nixon, Otis (OF)	1984–87
Nixon, Russ (C)	1957–60
Noboa, Junior (2B)	1984, 1987
Noles, Dickie (P)	1986
Norris, Jim (OF)	1977–79
Nunamaker, Leslie (C)	1919–22

O

O'Brien, Jack (OF)	1901
O'Brien, Pete (1B)	1989
O'Brien, Peter (IF)	1907
O'Dea, Paul (OF)	1944–45
Odenwald, Ted (P)	1921–22
Odom, John (P)	1975
O'Donoghue, John (P)	1966–67
Oelkers, Bryan (P)	1986
Ogea, Chad (P)	1994–98
O'Hagen, Harry (1B)	1902
Ojeda, Bobby (P)	1993
Olin, Steve (P)	1989–92
Oliver, Dave (2B)	1977
Olson, Gregg (P)	1995
Olson, Ivan (IF)	1911–14
O'Neill, Steve (C)	1911–23
Onslow, Edward (OF)	1918
Orosco, Jesse (P)	1989–91
Orta, Jorge (OF)	1980–81
Ortiz, Junior (C)	1992–93

Ostdiek, Henry (C)	1904	Peterson, Cap (OF)	1969
Otis, Harry (P)	1909	Peterson, Fritz (P)	1974–76
Otto, Dave (P)	1991–92	Petty, Jess (P)	1921
Oulliber, John (OF)	1933	Pezold, Larry (3B)	1914
Owchinko, Bob (P)	1980	Phelps, Josh (1B)	2004
		Phelps, Ken (1B)	1990
P		Philley, Dave (OF)	1954–55
Padgett, Ernie (3B)	1926–27	Phillips, Adolfo (OF)	1972
Pagel, Karl (1B)	1981–83	Phillips, Brandon (2B)	2002–05
Paige, George (P)	1911	Phillips, Bubba (3B, OF)	1960–62
Paige, Satchel (P)	1948–49	Phillips, Ed (C)	1935
Palmer, Lowell (P)	1972	Phillips, Jason (P)	2002–03
Papish, Frank (P)	1949	Phillips, Thomas (P)	1919
Parker, Harry (P)	1976	Pickering, Ollie (OF)	1901–02
Paronto, Chad (P)	2002–03	Pieretti, Marino (P)	1950
Parrish, Lance (C)	1993	Piersall, Jim (OF)	1959–61
Parsons, Casey (—)	1987	Pina, Horacio (P)	1968–69
Paschal, Ben (—)	1915	Piniella, Lou (OF)	1968
Pascual, Camilo (P)	1971	Pinson, Vada (OF, 1B)	1970–71
Paul, Mike (P)	1968–71	Pitula, Stan (P)	1957
Pawloski, Stan (2B)	1955	Pizarro, Juan (P)	1969
Paxton, Mike (P)	1978–80	Plunk, Eric (P)	1992–98
Pearson, Alexander (P)	1903	Poat, Ray (P)	1942–44
Pearson, Monte (P)	1932–35	Podbielan, Bud (P)	1959
Peck, Hal (OF)	1947–49	Podgajny, John (P)	1946
Peckinpaugh, Roger (SS)	1910, 1912–13	Polchow, Louis (P)	1902
Pena, Geronimo (3B, 2B)	1996	Poole, Jim (P)	1995–96, 1998–99
Pena, Orlando (P)	1967	Pope, Dave (OF)	1952, 1954–56
Peña, Tony (C)	1994–96	Porter, Dick (OF, 2B)	1929–34
Penner, Kenneth (P)	1916	Porter, J.W. (C)	1958
Peralta, Jhonny (SS)	2003–06	Post, Wally (OF)	1964
Perconte, Jack (2B)	1982–83	Pote, Lou (P)	2004
Perez, Eddie (C)	2002	Pott, Nelson (P)	1922
Perez, Rafael (P)	2006	Pounds, William (P)	1903
Perezchica, Tony (3B, SS)	1991–92	Powell, John (1B)	1975–76
Perkins, Broderick (1B, OF)	1983–84	Power, Ted (P)	1992–93
Perlman, Jon (P)	1988	Power, Vic (IF)	1958–61
Perrin, William (P)	1934	Powers, Ellis (OF)	1932–33
Perring, George (3B, SS)	1908–10	Powers, John (OF)	1960
Perry, Chan (OF)	2000	Price, John (SS)	1946
Perry, Gaylord (P)	1972–75	Pruitt, Ron (OF, C, 3B)	1976–81
Perry, Herbert (1B, 3B)	1994–96	Pytlak, Frank (C)	1932–40
Perry, Jim (P)	1959–63, 1974–75		
Peters, John (C)	1918	**Q**	
Peters, Russ (IF)	1940–44, 1946	Quirk, Jamie (P)	1984

R

Rabbitt, Joe (OF)	1922
Radatz, Dick (P)	1966–67
Radinsky, Scott (P)	2001
Raftery, Thomas (OF)	1909
Ragland, Tom (2B)	1973
Raich, Eric (P)	1975–76
Raines, Larry (IF)	1957–58
Rakers, Jason (P)	1998–99
Ramirez, Alex (OF)	1998–2000
Ramirez, Manny (OF)	1993–2000
Ramos, Domingo (2B)	1988
Ramos, Pedro (P)	1962–64
Rath, Morris (3B)	1910
Reed, Jerry (P)	1982–83, 1985
Reed, Steve (P)	1998–2001
Regalado, Rudy (3B)	1954–56
Reich, Herman (OF)	1949
Reilley, Alex (OF)	1909
Reilly, Thomas (—)	1914
Reinholz, Arthur (3B)	1928
Reiser, Pete (OF)	1952
Reisigl, Jacob (P)	1911
Reuschel, Paul (P)	1978–79
Reynolds, Allie (P)	1942–46
Reynolds, Bob (P)	1975
Rhoads, Robert (P)	1903–09
Rhodes, Arthur (P)	2005
Rhomberg, Kevin (OF)	1982–84
Rice, Edgar (OF)	1934
Riddleberger, Denny (P)	1972
Ridzik, Steve (P)	1958
Rigdon, Paul (P)	2000
Riggan, Jerrod (P)	2002–03
Rincon, Ricardo (P)	1999–2002
Ripken, Billy (2B)	1995
Riske, David (P)	1999–2005
Ritter, Reggie (P)	1986–87
Rittwage, Jim (P)	1970
Roa, Joe (P)	1995–96
Robbins, Jake (P)	2004–05
Roberts, Bip (2B, OF)	1997
Roberts, Dave (OF)	1999–2001
Robertson, Jeriome (P)	2004
Robinson, Eddie (1B)	1942, 1946–48, 1957

Robinson, Frank (—)	1974–76
Robinson, Humberto (P)	1959
Rocco, Mickey (1B)	1943–46
Rocker, John (P)	2001
Rodgers, Wilbur (2B)	1915
Rodriguez, Nerio (P)	2002
Rodriguez, Ricardo (P)	2002–03
Rodriguez, Rich (P)	2001
Rodriguez, Rick (P)	1988
Rohde, Dave (3B)	1992
Rohn, Dan (2B, 3B)	1986
Rohr, Billy (P)	1968
Rollins, Rich (3B)	1970
Roman, Jose (P)	1984–86
Romano, John (C)	1960–64
Romero, Ramon (P)	1984–85
Romo, Vicente (P)	1968–69
Roof, Phil (C)	1965
Rosar, Buddy (C)	1943–44
Rosello, Dave (IF)	1979–81
Rosen, Al (3B, 1B)	1947–56
Rosenthal, Larry (OF)	1941
Ross, Don (3B)	1945–46
Rossman, Claude (1B, OF)	1904, 1906
Roth, Robert (OF)	1915–18
Rothel, Robert (3B)	1945
Roy, Luther (P)	1924–25
Rozek, Dick (P)	1950–52
Rudolph, Don (P)	1962
Ruhle, Vern (P)	1985
Russell, Jack (P)	1932
Russell, Jeff (P)	1994
Russell, Lloyd (—)	1938
Ruszkowski, Hank (C)	1944–45, 1947
Rutherford, Jim (OF)	1910
Ryan, Buddy (OF)	1912–13
Ryan, Jack (P)	1908

S

Sabathia, C.C. (P)	2001–06
Sadler, Carl (P)	2002–03
Salas, Mark (—)	1989
Salmon, Chico (IF, OF)	1964–68
Salveson, John (P)	1943, 1945
Sanders, Ken (P)	1973–74

Santana, Rafael (SS)	1990	Sizemore, Grady (OF)	2004–06
Santiago, Jose G. (P)	1954–55	Skalski, Joe (P)	1989
Santiago, Jose R. (P)	2003	Skinner, Joel (C)	1989–91
Santos, Angel (2B)	2003	Slattery, John (1B)	1903
Sauerbeck, Scott (P)	2005–06	Slocum, Brian (P)	2006
Schaefer, Herman (2B)	1918	Slocumb, Heathcliff (P)	1993
Schaffernoth, Joe (P)	1961	Smiley, John (P)	1997
Schatzeder, Dan (P)	1988	Smith, Al (OF, 3B)	1953–57, 1964
Scheibeck, Frank (SS)	1901	Smith, Alfred (P)	1940–45
Scheinblum, Richie (OF)	1965, 1967–69	Smith, Charles (P)	1902
Schlueter, Norman (C)	1944	Smith, Clarence (P)	1916–17
Schreckengost, Ossee (1B)	1902	Smith, Clay (P)	1938
Schrom, Ken (P)	1986–87	Smith, Elmer (OF)	1914–17, 1919–21
Schulze, Don (P)	1984–86	Smith, Robert (P)	1959
Schwartz, William (1B)	1904	Smith, Roy (P)	1984–85
Score, Herb (P)	1955–59	Smith, Sherrod (P)	1922–27
Scott, Ed (P)	1901	Smith, Syd (C)	1910–11
Scudder, Scott (P)	1992–93	Smith, Tommy (OF)	1973–76
Seanez, Rudy (P)	1989–91	Smith, W. Roy (P)	2001–02
Seeds, Robert (OF)	1930–32, 1934	Smith, Willie (1B, OF)	1967–68
Seerey, Pat (OF)	1943–48	Snyder, Cory (OF, SS, 3B)	1986–90
Segui, David (1B)	2000	Snyder, Earl (1B, OF)	2002
Seitzer, Kevin (1B, 3B)	1996–97	Snyder, Russ (OF)	1968–69
Selby, Bill (3B, OF)	2000, 2002–03	Sodd, William (—)	1937
Sepkowski, Ted (2B, 3B)	1942, 1946–47	Solters, Julius (OF)	1937–39
Sewell, Joe (IF)	1920–30	Sorensen, Lary (P)	1982–83
Sewell, Luke (C)	1921–32, 1939	Sorensen, Zach (2B)	2003
Sexson, Richie (1B, OF)	1997–2000	Sorrells, Ray (SS)	1922
Seyfried, Gordon (P)	1963–64	Sorrento, Paul (1B)	1992–95
Shaner, Walter (OF)	1923	Sothoron, Allen (P)	1921–22
Shaute, Joe (P)	1922–30	Southworth, William (OF)	1913, 1915
Shaw, Jeff (P)	1990–92	Sowers, Jeremy (P)	2006
Shay, Danny (SS)	1901	Speaker, Tris (OF)	1916–26
Sheaffer, Danny (—)	1989	Speece, Byron (P)	1925–26
Shields, Francis (1B)	1915	Speed, Horace (OF)	1978–79
Shilling, James (2B)	1939	Speier, Justin (P)	2000–01
Shinault, Enoch (C)	1921–22	Spencer, Roy (C)	1933–34
Shipke, William (2B)	1906	Spencer, Shane (OF)	2003
Shoffner, Milburn (P)	1929–31	Spikes, Charlie (OF)	1973–77
Shoppach, Kelly (C)	2006	Spillner, Dan (P)	1978–84
Shuey, Paul (P)	1994–2002	Spradlin, Jerry (P)	1999
Siebert, Sonny (P)	1964–69	Spring, Jack (P)	1965
Sikorski, Brian (P)	2006	Springer, Steve (3B)	1990
Simpson, Harry (OF, 1B)	1951–53, 1955	Sprinz, Joe (C)	1930–31
Sims, Duke (C, 1B, OF)	1964–70	Spurgeon, Fred (2B, 3B)	1924–27
Sitton, Carl (P)	1909	Stanford, Jason (P)	2003–06

Stange, Lee (P)	1964–66	Tasby, Willie (OF)	1962–63
Stanley, Fred (SS)	1971–72	Taubensee, Eddie (C)	1991, 2001
Stanton, Mike (P)	1980–81	Tavarez, Julian (P)	1993–96
Stark, Monroe (SS)	1909	Tavener, John (SS)	1929
Starnagle, George (C)	1902	Taylor, Luther (P)	1902
Steen, Bill (P)	1912–15	Taylor, Ron (P)	1962
Steiner, Jim (C)	1945	Taylor, Sam (C)	1963
Stephens, Bryan (P)	1947	Tebbetts, Birdie (C)	1951–52
Stephenson, Riggs (2B, 3B, OF)	1921–25	Tedrow, Allen (P)	1914
Stevens, Dave (P)	1999	Temple, John (2B, 3B)	1960–61
Stevens, Lee (1B, OF)	2002	Terry, Ralph (P)	1965
Stewart, Sammy (P)	1987	Thielman, John (P)	1907–08
Stewart, Scott (P)	2004	Thomas, Carl (P)	1960
Stewart, Walter (P)	1935	Thomas, Chester (C)	1918–21
Stigman, Dick (P)	1960–61	Thomas, Fay (P)	1931
Stirnweiss, George (2B)	1951–52	Thomas, Gorman (OF)	1983
Stoddard, Tim (P)	1989	Thomas, Stan (P)	1976
Stovall, George (IF, OF)	1904–11	Thomas, Valmy (C)	1961
Stovall, Jesse (P)	1903	Thomason, Arthur (OF)	1910
Streit, Oscar (P)	1902	Thome, Jim (3B, 1B)	1991–2002
Strickland, George (IF)	1952–57, 1959–60	Thompson, Rich (P)	1985
Strickland, Jim (P)	1975	Thompson, Ryan (OF)	1996
Striker, Jake (P)	1959	Thoney, Jack (OF, 2B, SS)	1902–03
Strom, Brent (P)	1973	Thornton, Andre (1B)	1977–79, 1981–87
Stromme, Floyd (P)	1939	Tiant, Luis (P)	1964–69
Suarez, Ken (C)	1968–69, 1971	Tidrow, Dick (P)	1972–74
Suche, Charles (P)	1938	Tiefenauer, Bob (P)	1960, 1965, 1967
Sudakis, Bill (1B)	1975	Timmerman, Tom (P)	1973–74
Sullivan, Dennis (OF)	1908–09	Tingley, Ron (C)	1988
Sullivan, James (P)	1923	Tipton, Joe (C)	1948, 1952–53
Sullivan, Paul (P)	1939	Tolson, Charles (1B)	1925
Sullivan, William (C)	1936–37	Tomanek, Dick (P)	1953–54, 1957–58
Summa, Homer (OF)	1922–28	Torkelson, Chester (P)	1917
Susce, George (C)	1941–44	Torres, Rosendo (OF)	1973–74
Sutcliffe, Rick (P)	1982–84	Townsend, Jack (P)	1906
Sutherland, Darrell (P)	1968	Traber, Billy (P)	2003
Swan, Russ (P)	1994	Treadway, Jeff (3B, 2B)	1993
Swindell, Greg (P)	1986–91, 1996	Tresh, Mike (C)	1949
Swindell, Joshua (P)	1911, 1913	Trillo, Manny (2B)	1983
		Trosky, Hal (1B)	1933–41
T		Trouppe, Quincy (C)	1952
Tabler, Pat (1B, OF, 3B)	1983–88	Tucker, Ollie (OF)	1928
Tadano, Kazuhito (P)	2004–05	Tucker, Scooter (C)	1995
Tallet, Brian (P)	2002–03, 2005	Tucker, Thurman (OF)	1948–51
Tam, Jeff (P)	1999	Turchin, Edward (3B)	1943
Tanner, Chuck (OF)	1959–60	Turner, Chris (C)	1999

Turner, Matt (P)	1994	Wakefield, Howard (C)	1905, 1907
Turner, Terry (IF, OF)	1904–18	Walker, Edward (P)	1902–03
Tyriver, Dave (P)	1962	Walker, Fred (P)	1912
		Walker, Gerald (OF)	1941
U		Walker, James (P)	1912, 1915
Uhlaender, Ted (OF)	1970–71	Walker, Jerry (P)	1963–64
Uhle, George (P)	1919–28, 1936	Walker, Mike (P)	1988, 1990–91
Ujdur, Jerry (P)	1984	Walters, Al (C)	1924–25
Underhill, Vern (P)	1927–28	Wambsganss, William (2B, SS, 3B)	1914–23
Unser, Dell (OF)	1972	Ward, Aaron (3B)	1928
Upp, George (P)	1909	Ward, Colby (P)	1990
Upshaw, Cecil (P)	1974	Ward, Preston (1B, 3B, OF)	1956–58
Upshaw, Willie (1B)	1988	Ward, Turner (OF)	1990–91
Usher, Bob (OF)	1957	Wardle, Curt (P)	1985
Ussat, Bill (3B)	1925, 1927	Wasdell, Jim (1B)	1946–47
		Washington, Ron (SS)	1988
V		Watson, Mark (P)	2000
Vail, Mike (OF)	1978	Wayenberg, Frank (P)	1924
Valdez, Efrain (P)	1990–91	Weatherly, Roy (OF)	1936–42
Valdez, Sergio (P)	1990–91	Weathers, Dave (P)	1997
Valentinetti, Vito (P)	1957	Weaver, Floyd (P)	1962, 1965
Valo, Elmer (OF)	1959	Webb, James (SS)	1938–39
Van Camp, Al (1B)	1928	Webber, Les (P)	1946, 1948
Vande Berg, Ed (P)	1987	Webster, Mitch (OF)	1990–91
Vander Meer, John (P)	1951	Webster, Ray (2B)	1959
Varney, Lawrence (P)	1902	Weigel, Ralph(C)	1946
Vasbinder, M. Calhoun (P)	1902	Weik, Dick (P)	1950, 1953
Vazquez, Ramon (3B)	2005–06	Weiland, Robert (P)	1934
Velez, Otto (—)	1983	Weingartner, Elmer (SS)	1945
Vernon, Mickey (1B)	1949–50, 1958	Welf, Oliver (—)	1916
Versalles, Zoilo (2B, 3B)	1969	Wensloff, Charles (P)	1948
Veryzer, Tom (SS)	1978–81	Wertz, Bill (P)	1993–94
Vidal, Jose (OF)	1966–68	Wertz, Vic (1B, OF)	1954–58
Villone, Ron (P)	1998	West, James (P)	1905, 1911
Vinson, Ernest (OF)	1904–05	Westbrook, Jake (P)	2001–06
Vizcaino, Jose (2B, SS)	1996	Westlake, Wally (OF)	1952–55
Vizquel, Omar (SS)	1994–2004	Weyhing, August (P)	1901
Von Ohlen, Dave (P)	1985	Wheeler, Ed (3B, SS)	1945
Vosmik, Joe (OF)	1930–36	Whisenant, Pete (OF)	1960
Vukovich, George (OF)	1983–85	White, Rick (P)	2004
		Whitehill, Earl (P)	1937–38
W		Whiten, Mark (OF)	1991–92, 1998–2000
Waddell, Tom (P)	1984–85, 1987	Whitfield, Fred (1B)	1963–67
Wagner, Leon (OF)	1964–68	Whitson, Ed (P)	1982
Wagner, Paul (P)	1999	Wickander, Kevin (P)	1989–90, 1992–93
Waits, Rick (P)	1975–83	Wickman, Bob (P)	2000–02, 2004–06

Wight, Bill (P)	1953, 1955
Wihtol, Sandy (P)	1979–80, 1982
Wilcox, Milt (P)	1972–74
Wilhelm, Hoyt (P)	1957–58
Wilie, Denney (OF)	1915
Wilkins, Eric (P)	1979
Wilkinson, Roy (P)	1918
Wilks, Ted (P)	1952–53
Willard, Jerry (C)	1984–85
Williams, Alva (1B)	1918
Williams, Brian (P)	2000
Williams, Dick (OF, 3B)	1957
Williams, Eddie (3B)	1986–88
Williams, Fred (1B)	1945
Williams, Matt (3B)	1997
Williams, Reggie (OF)	1988
Williams, Stan (P)	1965, 1967–69
Williams, Walt (OF)	1973
Willis, Les (P)	1947
Wills, Frank (P)	1986–87
Wilson, Arthur (C)	1921
Wilson, Enrique (3B, SS, 2B)	1997–2000
Wilson, Francis (—)	1928
Wilson, Jim (1B)	1985
Wilson, Nigel (OF)	1996
Wilson, Red (C)	1960
Winchell, Fred (P)	1909
Winegarner, Ralph (P)	1930, 1932, 1934–36
Winfield, Dave (—)	1995
Winn, George (P)	1922–23
Wise, Rick (P)	1978–79
Witt, Bobby (P)	2000
Wohlers, Mark (P)	2002
Wojna, Ed (P)	1989
Wolf, Ernest (P)	1912
Wolff, Roger (P)	1947
Wood, Joe (OF, 2B)	1917–22

Wood, Robert (C, 1B)	1901–02
Wood, Roy (OF, 1B)	1914–15
Woodard, Steve (P)	2000–01
Woodeshick, Hal (P)	1958
Woodling, Gene (OF)	1943, 1946, 1955–57
Workman, Charles (OF)	1938, 1941
Worrell, Tim (P)	1998
Worthington, Craig (3B)	1992
Wright, Albert (OF)	1935
Wright, Clarence (P)	1902–03
Wright, Jaret (P)	1997–2002
Wright, William (P)	1909
Wyatt, Loral (OF)	1924
Wyatt, Whitlow (P)	1937
Wynn, Early (P)	1949–57, 1963

Y

Yeager, George (C)	1901
Yett, Rich (P)	1986–89
Yingling, Earl (P)	1911
York, Michael (P)	1991
Yoter, Elmer (3B)	1924
Young, Bobby (2B)	1955–56
Young, Cliff (P)	1993
Young, Cy (P)	1909–11
Young, Ernie (—)	2004
Young, George (—)	1913
Young, Matt (P)	1993
Young, Mike (—)	1989
Yowell, Carl (P)	1924–25

Z

Zinn, James (P)	1929
Zoldak, Sam (P)	1948–50
Zuber, William (P)	1936, 1938–40
Zuvella, Paul (SS)	1988–89
Zuverink, George (P)	1951–52

Notes

A Great Player, a Great Manager

"You've got a bad ballclub..." Lewis, Franklin, *The Cleveland Indians,* New York: G.P. Putnam's Sons, 1949, page 85.

"You haven't got any sore arm..." Lewis, Franklin, *The Cleveland Indians,* New York: G.P. Putnam's Sons, 1949, page 127.

1920: From Tragedy to Triumph

"Coveleski pitched excellent ball today..." Staff Special, "Tribe's Hurlers Equal Dodgers', Speaker Says," *The* (Cleveland) *Plain Dealer,* October 6, 1920.

"I give Grimes the credit..." Staff Special, "Speaker Gives Grimes Credit for Box Work," *The* (Cleveland) *Plain Dealer,* October 7, 1920.

"The clubs are very evenly matched..." Staff Special, "Tris Confident, Repeats Tribe Is Sure to Win," *The* (Cleveland) *Plain Dealer,* October 8, 1920.

"It was one of the most remarkable games..." "Proud of Every Indian in Game, Spoke Declares," *The* (Cleveland) *Plain Dealer*, October 11, 1920.

"From the start, I never had any doubt..." "'I Knew It,' Said Speaker, as He Lauded Indians," *The* (Cleveland) *Plain Dealer,* October 13, 1920.

"Cleveland has a wonderful ballclub..." "Robinson Doffs Cap to Speaker and His Indians," *The* (Cleveland) *Plain Dealer,* October 13, 1920.

A Walk through the Parks

"When I first saw Jacobs Field..." Vizquel, Omar, *Omar! My Life On and Off the Field,* Cleveland: Gray and Company, 2002, page 73.

Starry, Starry Nights

"Foxx just about wrecked the game..." Alan Gould, Associated Press Sports Editor, "Frisch Says Walker Best of Tired Lot," *The* (Cleveland) *Plain Dealer,* July 9, 1935.

"I thought it was the best strategy..." Alan Gould, Associated Press Sports Editor, "Frisch Says Walker Best of Tired Lot," *The* (Cleveland) *Plain Dealer,* July 9, 1935.

"Practically all of them..." Alan Gould, Associated Press Sports Editor, "Frisch Says Walker Best of Tired Lot," *The* (Cleveland) *Plain Dealer,* July 9, 1935.

"I didn't sleep hardly a wink..." Chuck Heaton, "Sleepless Rosen 'Up' for Dream Game," *The* (Cleveland) *Plain Dealer,* July 14, 1954.

"There wasn't any question..." Chuck Heaton, "Sleepless Rosen 'Up' for Dream Game," *The* (Cleveland) *Plain Dealer,* July 14, 1954.

"Now they see..." Chuck Heaton, "Sleepless Rosen 'Up' for Dream Game," *The* (Cleveland) *Plain Dealer,* July 14, 1954.

"I don't care where you are..." Hal Lebovitz, "Mays Gets 'Go' Signal from Dark," *The* (Cleveland) *Plain Dealer,* July 10, 1963.

"I love to play ball..." Hal Lebovitz, "Mays Gets 'Go' Signal from Dark," *The* (Cleveland) *Plain Dealer,* July 10, 1963.

"Man, this fence..." Hal Lebovitz, "Mays Gets 'Go' Signal from Dark," *The* (Cleveland) *Plain Dealer,* July 10, 1963.

"I just had nothing..." Tony Grossi, "An All-Star's Nightmare," *The* (Cleveland) *Plain Dealer,* August 9, 1981.

"This was great..." Terry Pluto, "Record Crowd Sees NL Win Again," *The* (Cleveland) *Plain Dealer,* August 9, 1981.

"I felt like I was flying..." Paul Hoynes, "Sandy Steals the Show," *The* (Cleveland) *Plain Dealer,* July 9, 1997.

"I kept his hitting streak alive..." Paul Hoynes, "Hargrove Praises Alomar's Defense," *The* (Cleveland) *Plain Dealer,* July 10, 1997.

Mel Harder: A Long and Prosperous Career

"He helped me most by just talking..." Bob Dolgan, "Legendary Indians Pitcher, Coach Dies," *The* (Cleveland) *Plain Dealer,* October 21, 2002.

"His word was gospel," Bob Dolgan, "Legendary Indians Pitcher, Coach Dies," *The* (Cleveland) *Plain Dealer,* October 21, 2002.

"A right-handed pitcher of high-school age..." Lewis, Franklin, *The Cleveland Indians,* New York: G.P. Putnam's Sons, 1949, page 160.

"It's disappointing..." Bob Dolgan, "Enshrinement Eludes Harder Again," *The* (Cleveland) *Plain Dealer,* March 1, 2000.

"Mel Harder belongs..." Bill Livingston, "It Was Easy to Like Mel Harder," *The* (Cleveland) *Plain Dealer,* October 25, 2002.

Earl Averill: All He Did Was Hit

"Averill was the smallest..." Lewis, Franklin, *The Cleveland Indians,* New York: G.P. Putnam's Sons, 1949, page 162.

The Greatest Indian

"Gentlemen, I've found the greatest..." Lewis, Franklin, *The Cleveland Indians,* New York: G.P. Putnam's Sons, 1949, pages 190–191.

"Bob Feller's Recipe for a..." Feller, Bob, with Burton Rocks, *Bob Feller's Little Black Book of Baseball Wisdom,* Contemporary Books, Lincolnwood, Ill., 2001, page 109.

Lou Boudreau: The Boy Manager

"The more I inspected..." Boudreau, Lou, *Lou Boudreau: Covering All the Bases,* Champaign, Ill.: Sagamore Publishing, 1993, page 51.

"From that first minute..." Lewis, Franklin, *The Cleveland Indians,* New York: G.P. Putnam's Sons, 1949, page 219.

"Being made manager..." Lewis, Franklin, *The Cleveland Indians,* New York: G.P. Putnam's Sons, 1949, page 219.

"The season was a learning year..." Boudreau, Lou, *Lou Boudreau: Covering All the Bases,* Champaign, Ill.: Sagamore Publishing, 1993, page 64.

"From the moment..." Lewis, Franklin, *The Cleveland Indians,* New York: G.P. Putnam's Sons, 1949, page 205.

"Veeck was like a whirlwind..." Boudreau, Lou, *Lou Boudreau: Covering All the Bases,* Champaign, Ill.: Sagamore Publishing, 1993, page 80.

"I liked Louie..." Veeck, Bill, *Veeck—As in Wreck,* New York: Putnam, 1962, page 97.

"The acquisition of Larry Doby…" Moore, Thomas Joseph, *Pride against Prejudice: The Biography of Larry Doby*, Westport, Conn.: Greenwood Press, 1988, pages 42–43.

"Mr. Martin would have been proud…" Boudreau, Lou, *Lou Boudreau: Covering All the Bases*, Champaign, Ill.: Sagamore Publishing, 1993, page 125.

"The most remarkable thing…" Boudreau, Lou, *Lou Boudreau: Covering All the Bases*, Champaign, Ill.: Sagamore Publishing, 1993, page xii.

"Was Boudreau a better…" Bill Livingston, "A Producer and Director of Glory Lou Boudreau Did It All in 1948, Working Magic We Haven't Seen Since," *The* (Cleveland) *Plain Dealer*, August 11, 2001.

Larry Doby Makes History

"It was an emotional time…" Bob Dolgan, "Memories Stay Fresh: '48 Tribe Center Fielder Doby Emphasizes the Positive in a Storied Life of Bittersweet Baseball Experiences," *The* (Cleveland) *Plain Dealer*, May 31, 1998.

"Color was never an issue with me…" Bob Dolgan, "A Racial Milestone: Steve Gromek Won a World Series Game for the Tribe in 1948, but He Is Remembered for Hug He Gave Doby Celebrating the Win," *The* (Cleveland) *Plain Dealer*, April 26, 1998.

"I have always had a strong feeling for minority groups…" Veeck, Bill, *Veeck—As in Wreck*, New York: Putnam, 1962, page 171.

"He was one of the greatest people…" Bob Dolgan, "Tribe Great Larry Doby Dies: First Black Player in American League," *The* (Cleveland) *Plain Dealer*, June 19, 2003.

"People are doing a lot of unnecessary guessing…" Gordon Cobbledick, "Plain Dealing: There's No Need to Guess about Larry Doby; He Will Be Accepted if He Proves Big Leaguer," *The* (Cleveland) *Plain Dealer*, July 6, 1947.

"For Larry Doby…" Moore, Thomas Joseph, *Pride against Prejudice: The Biography of Larry Doby*, Westport, Conn.: Greenwood Press, 1988, page 50.

"When I first went to bat in Chicago..." Moore, Thomas Joseph, *Pride against Prejudice: The Biography of Larry Doby,* Westport, Conn.: Greenwood Press, 1988, page 57.

"It was one of the toughest things..." Bob Dolgan, "Tribe Great Larry Doby Dies: First Black Player in American League," *The* (Cleveland) *Plain Dealer,* June 19, 2003.

"Number of players enshrined in the Baseball Hall..." from Indians 2006 Information and Records Book.

"I'm happy with the career I had..." Bob Dolgan, "Tribe Great Larry Doby Dies: First Black Player in American League," *The* (Cleveland) *Plain Dealer,* June 19, 2003.

"Life is too short for that..." Bob Dolgan, "Tribe Great Larry Doby Dies: First Black Player in American League," *The* (Cleveland) *Plain Dealer,* June 19, 2003.

"He was a keystone..." Paul Hoynes, "Larry Doby Was 'Keystone' to Team's History, Says Dolan," *The* (Cleveland) *Plain Dealer,* June 19, 2003.

"He was a great American..." MLB.com, June 19, 2003.

1948: Champions at Last

"It was a tough one..." Charles Heaton, "Looks Forward to Being 'Back at These Guys'" *The* (Cleveland) *Plain Dealer,* October 7, 1948.

"I'm sure that Masi was out..." Harry Jones, "Lemon Seeks to Tie Series Today," *The* (Cleveland) *Plain Dealer,* October 7, 1948.

"Still no prediction..." Charles Heaton, "Doubles, Scores Tying Run, Drives Another Across," *The* (Cleveland) *Plain Dealer,* October 8, 1948.

"The toughest thing for me..." Charles Heaton, "Doubles, Scores Tying Run, Drives Another Across," *The* (Cleveland) *Plain Dealer,* October 8, 1948.

"Always wanted Gene to be a pitcher..." Charles Heaton, "Gene Declares He's Ready to Pitch Today and Will Be in Bull Pen," *The* (Cleveland) *Plain Dealer,* October 9, 1948.

"We'll be back with Johnny Sain..." Charles Heaton, "Gene Declares He's Ready to Pitch Today and Will Be in Bull Pen," *The* (Cleveland) *Plain Dealer,* October 9, 1948.

"I didn't sleep much last night..." Charles Heaton, "Lack of Sleep Fails to Slow Down Gromek," *The* (Cleveland) *Plain Dealer,* October 10, 1948.

"What a relief to get some runs..." Charles Heaton, "'We're On Our Way,' Declares Braves' Elliott," *The* (Cleveland) *Plain Dealer,* October 11, 1948.

"Oh, I was tired..." Charles Heaton, "Gene Plays Big Role in 10-Day Drive to Title," *The* (Cleveland) *Plain Dealer,* October 12, 1948.

"It was Bearden's series..." Charles Heaton, "Gene Plays Big Role in 10-Day Drive to Title," *The* (Cleveland) *Plain Dealer,* October 12, 1948.

No Sweeter Guy Than Bob Lemon

"He made the change so easy..." Bob Dolgan, "Indians Recall 'Great Teammate,'" *The* (Cleveland) *Plain Dealer,* January 13, 2000.

"It was with tremendous sadness..." Bob Dolgan, "Indians Recall 'Great Teammate,'" *The* (Cleveland) *Plain Dealer,* January 13, 2000.

1954: Surprising Sweep

"I'd been holding Rhodes..." Dan Cordtz, "Durocher Declares He Was Saving Rhodes," *The* (Cleveland) *Plain Dealer,* September 30, 1954.

"I wasn't trying for a home run..." Dan Cordtz, "Durocher Declares He Was Saving Rhodes," *The* (Cleveland) *Plain Dealer,* September 30, 1954.

"I slowed down when I started..." Dan Cordtz, "Durocher Declares He Was Saving Rhodes," *The* (Cleveland) *Plain Dealer,* September 30, 1954.

"I can only say that it was one of the greatest..." Dan Cordtz, "Durocher Declares He Was Saving Rhodes," *The* (Cleveland) *Plain Dealer,* September 30, 1954.

"They got their hits when it counted..." International News Service, "Series Clubhouses Quotes," *The* (Cleveland) *Plain Dealer,* October 1, 1954.

"I ain't thinking about no records..." Dan Cordtz, "Rhodes Ties Record," *The* (Cleveland) *Plain Dealer,* October 2, 1954.

"There was never any question..." Joe Reichler, "'No Team Could Have Beaten Us,' Says Dark," *The* (Cleveland) *Plain Dealer,* October 3, 1954.

"They played championship baseball..." Dan Cordtz, "Lopez Offers No Excuses," *The* (Cleveland) *Plain Dealer,* October 3, 1954.

A Winning Score

"As soon as I hit the ground..." Bob Dolgan, "A Sickening Thud," *The* (Cleveland) *Plain Dealer,* May 6, 1997.

"I've been in pain before..." Bob Dolgan, "A Sickening Thud," *The* (Cleveland) *Plain Dealer,* May 6, 1997.

Was Gaylord Perry All Wet?

"Gaylord, it's time to try it out..." Perry, Gaylord, *Me and the Spitter,* New York: E.P. Dutton, 1974, page 14.

"That look of pride you get..." Perry, Gaylord, *Me and the Spitter,* New York: E.P. Dutton, 1974, page 19.

"During the next eight years..." Perry, Gaylord, *Me and the Spitter,* New York: E.P. Dutton, 1974, page 12.

"Three slippery elm tablets to suck on..." Perry, Gaylord, *Me and the Spitter,* New York: E.P. Dutton, 1974, page 30.

"I never wanted to be out there without anything..." Perry, Gaylord, *Me and the Spitter,* New York: E.P. Dutton, 1974, page 32.

Cleveland Makes History Again

"I think it would have been one of Jackie's biggest thrills..." Associated Press, "Jackie's Widow Happy," *The* (Cleveland) *Plain Dealer,* October 4, 1974.

"The impact of Frank Robinson..." Russell Schneider, "Long Overdue, Says Calm Kuhn," *The* (Cleveland) *Plain Dealer,* October 4, 1974.

"I don't know if I could go through..." Russell Schneider, "Pitching Top Need, Says Robbie," *The* (Cleveland) *Plain Dealer,* October 4, 1974.

"I'm the first one only because..." Russell Schneider, "Pitching Top Need, Says Robbie," *The* (Cleveland) *Plain Dealer,* October 4, 1974.

546 NOTES

"I don't see any problem in firing me..." Russell Schneider, "Pitching Top Need, Says Robbie," The (Cleveland) Plain Dealer, October 4, 1974.

"Frank Robinson is here because..." Russell Schneider, "Pitching Top Need, Says Robbie," The (Cleveland) Plain Dealer, October 4, 1974.

"I'm not resentful of anything..." Staff Special (Russ Schneider), "Disappointed Doby Is Not Vindictive," The (Cleveland) Plain Dealer, October 3, 1974.

"Frank Robinson is a man..." Hal Lebovitz, "Robbie...His Time Has Come," The (Cleveland) Plain Dealer, October 3, 1974.

"I'm delighted somebody..." Dennis Lustig, "Reaction Generally Favorable," The (Cleveland) Plain Dealer, October 3, 1974.

"Frank is definitely ready..." Dennis Lustig, "Reaction Generally Favorable," The (Cleveland) Plain Dealer, October 3, 1974.

"I think it's a hell of a move..." Russell Schneider, "Tribe Players Endorse Robbie," The (Cleveland) Plain Dealer, October 3, 1974.

"If he manages the way he played..." Russell Schneider, "Tribe Players Endorse Robbie," The (Cleveland) Plain Dealer, October 3, 1974.

"It doesn't make any difference," Russell Schneider, "Tribe Players Endorse Robbie," The (Cleveland) Plain Dealer, October 3, 1974.

"Any home run is a thrill..." Russell Schneider, "56,204 See Robby's Storybook Debut," The (Cleveland) Plain Dealer, April 9, 1975.

"Right now I feel better..." Bob Dyer, "Robinson Goes Deep into Baseball History; First Black Manager Debuts with Homer 30 Years Ago," Akron Beacon Journal, April 8, 2005.

"And even if you were frozen..." Hal Lebovitz, "Was It Fiction...?" The (Cleveland) Plain Dealer, April 9, 1975.

"It was the kind of a debut..." Russell Schneider, "56,204 See Robby's Storybook Debut," The (Cleveland) Plain Dealer, April 9, 1975.

"More and more I'm realizing..." Robinson, Frank, Frank: The First Year, New York: Holt, Rinehart and Winston, 1976, page 167.

"I like it better this way..." Robinson, Frank, Frank: The First Year, New York: Holt, Rinehart and Winston, 1976, page 167.

"I always did what I thought was right…" Schneider, Russell J., *Frank Robinson: The Making of a Manager,* New York: Coward, McCann & Geoghegan, Inc., 1976, pages 244–245.

"I'm not upset…" Schneider, Russell, *The Cleveland Indians Encyclopedia,* Third Edition, Champaign, Ill.: Sports Publishing LLC, 2004, page 343.

Mike Hargrove: The Most Popular Indian?

"Mike is very supportive…" Mary Kay Cabot, "The Many Faces of Sharon Hargrove," *The* (Cleveland) *Plain Dealer,* September 8, 1996.

"I was devastated…" Mary Kay Cabot, "The Many Faces of Sharon Hargrove," *The* (Cleveland) *Plain Dealer,* September 8, 1996.

Trials and Tribulations

"The news spread…" Henry P. Edwards, "Baseball World Mourns When It Learns of the Death of Addie Joss," *The* (Cleveland) *Plain Dealer,* April 15, 1911.

1995: Return to Glory

"I felt I wasn't the right man for the job…" Paul Hoynes, "Grounded in Atlanta, Fast Start, Slow Finish," *The* (Cleveland) *Plain Dealer,* October 22, 1995.

"That was about as well-pitched a game…" Paul Hoynes, "Grounded in Atlanta, Fast Start, Slow Finish," *The* (Cleveland) *Plain Dealer,* October 22, 1995.

"My game plan was to pitch around Lopez…" Paul Hoynes, "Tribe Misses Chances, Game 2 Slides Away," *The* (Cleveland) *Plain Dealer,* October 23, 1995.

"We told each other…" Paul Hoynes, "Murray Wins It in 11th, Jacobs Field Magic," *The* (Cleveland) *Plain Dealer,* October 25, 1995.

"Herbert made the play of the game…" Paul Hoynes, "Murray Wins It in 11th, Jacobs Field Magic," *The* (Cleveland) *Plain Dealer,* October 25, 1995.

"It's hard to beat anybody…" Paul Hoynes, "Backs to the Wall, Braves Win; Maddux Next," *The* (Cleveland) *Plain Dealer,* October 26, 1995.

"I think I may have overmanaged myself..." Paul Hoynes, "Alive and Sky High Tribe Solves Maddux," *The* (Cleveland) *Plain Dealer,* October 27, 1995.

"This was a good season..." Paul Hoynes, "Glavine Stifles Tribe, Oh, So Close," *The* (Cleveland) *Plain Dealer,* October 29, 1995.

Jim Thome: Super Slugger

"Look, I am a guy from Peoria..." Burt Graeff, "Power Numbers Put Thome in Some Powerful Company," *The* (Cleveland) *Plain Dealer,* October 8, 1999.

1997: Return Engagement

"There's no defense..." Paul Hoynes, "Marlins Pound Hershiser in Series Opener," *The* (Cleveland) *Plain Dealer,* October 19, 1997.

"Alomar had a big blow..." Paul Hoynes, "Ogea Ties 'Em Up," *The* (Cleveland) *Plain Dealer,* October 20, 1997.

"These things go in stages..." Paul Hoynes, "Ogea Ties 'Em Up," *The* (Cleveland) *Plain Dealer,* October 20, 1997.

"We didn't get good starting pitching..." Paul Hoynes, "Indians Fall Apart in Seven-Run Ninth," *The* (Cleveland) *Plain Dealer,* October 22, 1997.

"I pitched okay in the early innings..." Michelle Kaufman, "Twice Bitten Bulldog," *Miami Herald,* October 24, 1997.

"Our team has faced a lot..." Mike DiGiovanna, "Marlins Win in Alou-loo," *Los Angeles Times,* October 24, 1997.

"I was just trying to make contact..." Hal McCoy, "Tribe Forces a 7th Game," *Dayton Daily News,* October 26, 1997.

"It was the most important play..." Hal McCoy, "Tribe Forces a 7th Game," *Dayton Daily News,* October 26, 1997.

"I was getting a drink..." Hal McCoy, "Tribe Forces a 7th Game," *Dayton Daily News,* October 26, 1997.

"I can't tell you..." Paul Hoynes, "Marlins Win Game 7 in 11," *The* (Cleveland) *Plain Dealer,* October 27, 1997.

A Gold Glove Personality

"That would be awesome if they asked me..." Mary Schmitt Boyer, "'Little' Vizquel Has Big Impact," *The* (Cleveland) *Plain Dealer,*

June 10, 2002.

"It's not a subject you hear..." Mary Schmitt Boyer, "Political Arenas? Browns' Interest Greater Than Tribe's, Cavs'," *The* (Cleveland) *Plain Dealer,* October 29, 2004.

"The most important asset for a major league baseball player..." Vizquel, Omar, *Omar! My Life On and Off the Field,* Cleveland: Gray and Company, 2002, page 13.

"To my mom, whose love and dedication..." Vizquel, Omar, *Omar! My Life On and Off the Field,* Cleveland: Gray and Company, 2002, dedication page.

The Indians and the Arts

"In 1949 Gene Bearden played..." Davis, Marc, *Cleveland Indians Facts & Trivia,* South Bend, Ind.: E.B. Houchin Company, 1997, pages 227–228, 252.

"Take off the mask..." Ben Broussard, *Ben Broussard,* compact disc, © 2005 Lazy Bones Recordings, Inc.

"Roller coaster up and down..." Ben Broussard, *Ben Broussard,* compact disc, © 2005 Lazy Bones Recordings, Inc.

"I don't remember..." Pluto, Terry, *Our Tribe: A Baseball Memoir,* New York: Simon & Schuster, 1999, page 191.

"Baseball filled..." Pluto, Terry, *Our Tribe: A Baseball Memoir,* New York: Simon & Schuster, 1999, page 30.

"I'll always be..." Pluto, Terry, *Our Tribe: A Baseball Memoir,* New York: Simon & Schuster, 1999, page 250.

Looking to the Future

"Still, I didn't necessarily disagree..." Vizquel, Omar, *Omar! My Life On and Off the Field,* Cleveland: Gray and Company, 2002, page 130.